Simple Choices

*Thoughts on choosing environments that
support who your child is meant to be*

Lisa Graham Keegan

Copyright© 2013 by Lisa Graham Keegan

All rights reserved. No part of this publication may be reproduced, stored in a retrieval system or transmitted, in any form or by any means, electronic, mechanical, photocopying, recording or otherwise, without the prior permission of the copyright holder.

ISBN 978-0-9887451-0-0

Printed in the United States of America by Epic Print Solutions

Cover Design by Floyd Orfield

Table of Contents

~~~~

Foreword		*v*
Introduction		*ix*
Chapter One	A Chosen Path	*1*
Chapter Two	Choosing Motherhood	*19*
Chapter Three	Choice and Expectation	*29*
Chapter Four	The Choice of Fathers	*39*
Chapter Five	Mother's Choice	*59*
Chapter Six	Choosing an Adult Path	*67*
Chapter Seven	Guidepost One	*71*
Chapter Eight	Guidepost Two	*81*
Chapter Nine	Guidepost Three	*97*
Chapter Ten	Choosing the Future	*115*
About the Author		*129*

Dedication

To Pat Holtzapple Weinberg, my trusted butterfly.

Foreword

by
Annie Graham and Kate Keegan McClendon

―――――∞―――――

*O*ur family is epic. It's something we have explained to plenty of people, and we have watched lots of faces express confusion.

But in our family the happy fact is that we welcome the discussion. We try not to be congratulatory about ourselves, knowing that the facts of divorce and remarriage which created our family have caused irreconcilable divisions in many others. But it is our truth and we explain it, because it is an amazing thing.

Lisa (also known as Mom, or Ulee if you are one of two grandsons) works to allow individuals the right to make their own choices. As her daughter and stepdaughter we have seen her fight a battle for the right to choose excellent schools on behalf of millions across this country—for families she will never meet—and she has helped children in ways she will never know. She has often done it at a high personal cost to herself and her family as she fights for others.

But that is not just her story; it is the story of our family. Our immediate family is a mix of steps, exes, and in-laws that from the outside wouldn't seem to be cohesive. The commitment from all five of our parents created our beautiful blended family that spends holidays, vacations, meals and merriment together. Combining families after divorce is no easy task, but Lisa and the rest of our parents are as passionate about getting this right as they are about anything else in life.

This book was written by Lisa as one member of this massive family. She wrote to describe all of its members as gifts, and to make the point that families are the most important building blocks in a stable society. Though she does not have the ultimate insight of living in our heads for the past few decades, she knows our individual and collective stories very well. Acknowledging the strength of her perspective, we believe that people will see undeniable truths here, and the perseverance of this family to be just that—a family in the face of anything—is one of them.

We have four other brothers in our family, and we both stopped adding the prefix step- or half- when telling stories from our family life years ago. When people prod or ask why the gap in our ages exists, we can provide this answer: "They are my step-siblings," but leaving out the prefix fits the highest and best nature of our nuclear family that persists, despite all the changes over the years. Because there are so many members of this family it can be difficult to stay in touch with everyone. But the same is true for anyone we know in this life. Space and time apart do not reflect animosity; they are merely indicators of the fact that there is only so much time in a day, and for us, only so many times we can master the logistics of putting together a party of 50 relatives.

In our family, we have the honor of bearing witness to and being the beneficiaries of our parents' work. And of seeing how their work becomes very personal. This past year Kate's son (Lisa's grandson) Aidan started attending a charter school made possible by Lisa's work in the legislature almost 20 years ago. He was fortunate to get into it because this school is now frequently recognized as best in the country—not just for charter schools, but for all schools, public or private. It has become so popular that there are far more applicants than can attend. Aidan was put into the lottery for a place in the school just as all prospective students for this school must be, hoping to get a chance at an education that could change the trajectory of their lives.

It felt bizarre. After all of Lisa's work in fighting for school reforms, writing the law that created Arizona's charter schools and lobbying for decision makers to consider the weight of their votes—after all of this she stood helplessly awaiting the random lottery results, as any other concerned parent or grandparent must do. Aidan had been in a good school and he would have stayed there had the luck of the draw not favored him. Chance made the difference between good and exceptional for Lisa's grandson.

This fight is real for her.

She has been our family's champion as well. Sometimes that is difficult, just as in all other collections of people who are inextricably bound together. But there is a lot of love in this group, and it seems that we've always recognized the need to share it.

No, this is not a "Leave it to Beaver" family. Of course not; thank goodness. But we are a family created by all of us making the choice to be one; and together, we support the potential each of us was created to offer.

Introduction

Finally, as of this year, all of my children are officially adults—as defined by the calendar and by their behavior—thank God. And whew.

So I get to say things beyond the public policy and electoral constraints that have defined my writing for decades. Because while both my husband and I have spent a lifetime in the public arena, we tried to spare our children a blurring of the lines between what our public and private selves said when they were young. Mostly we avoided saying much about the children themselves other than they are wonderful and we love them. Which they are and we do.

But our kids are now old enough and sage enough to manage a little personal disclosure by their parents. Plus it's the great revenge of advancing age—extracting the same kind of cringing from our children that they extracted from us.

Sidebar favorite example of the above: My nephew telling his teacher that the picture of a blender she was holding up in front of the class was "a cocktail machine!"

Our children can make us sound a lot more fun than we really are. My sister had some credibility issues after my nephew's revelation.

Anyway.

Years ago, I thought, "When all the kids are real live grown-ups, I am going to write a book so moms will understand what school choice really means and why they should go get some!"

Awesome idea. So I started that book by describing my belief in the inherent value of each unique child and how their talents can flourish under the leadership of uniquely talented teachers. Which led me to address current education policies and how we prevent teachers from reaching the very unique children in the world. And that of course meant I needed to explain how those bad policy ideas became enshrined in the first place, and why they must be changed. And that required a discussion of how it is possible to change the law. So I shared my experience with writing and helping to pass laws that allow teachers to create and offer schools that parents may choose for their children. And having arrived at that point, I realized that I was basically writing the book backwards, and not dealing with first principles.

Which was sort of an alarming discovery, but books really do want to tell their own story. So this bossy book pushed that one aside, and all of those really good ideas are gently swathed in plastic wrap for the moment, cooling and marinating. Because as important as all of that is, the detail is secondary to the magnitude of the hopes and dreams and responsibilities I hold for all of our children.

Children are everything. Their arrival destroys any prior view of the world, and orients us toward the future. Any meaningful connection to a child makes each of us tangibly responsible for what happens next. Everyone should want children to know the great joys of life...the relationships, the ideas, the learning of lessons and the struggles involved to make a better world. And all children should be well prepared to make their own contribution.

And I do mean THEIR contribution. Supporting who children are *as individuals* means making the best choices for their lives ahead, as adults. The fact is this: choice on behalf of children must be specific to them. Children come to this world with a diversity of talents, hopes and aspirations. Each individual arrives with a unique orientation and in a specific family environment. Experiences that shape the soul are life's lessons in choice—and those lessons either contract and limit us, or they teach us how to expand, to improve and to be all that we are capable of becoming.

And that is first principle.

My family taught me that the contributions a child can make to his or her loved ones, community, country and world are to be valued beyond measure. And, as I was taught, I hope for everyone to take responsibility for the children who cross our paths. Recognize and support their unique gifts. Push them to excel by choosing for them the experiences and environments that will best teach and inspire. Realize that society *depends* on how children are raised and educated, and society *reflects* how children are raised and educated.

So my work on the issue of school choice is borne of a much more essential and personal view of how all people matter to one another. We can only diminish the risk of an irreparable divide between those with limited choice and those with expansive choice by building a society where all children are taught to know and love themselves as unique individuals who may easily and joyfully find their way to belong to, serve and enjoy their communities. I believe with all my heart that such a society is possible.

I am unable to write a book solely about school choice yet. I don't want to promote something that matters so intensely before sharing the life circumstances, choices and decisions that made my commitment to school choice such an essential piece of who I am. What I have learned from my political life is that no one is completely intellectually consistent. People tend to like what their trusted allies and friends like.

So I wanna be your friend!!!

Okay, that's shallow. We can wait and see how you feel about the whole friendship thing. You may discover a few things in this book that make friendship with me risky for you. But I think an honest way to make sense of complex issues is to tell a simpler story. I love stories and I am grateful for mine.

My life's work has been to make sure all people can choose the best education possible for their own children or the children in their care/neighborhood/universe. I have worked on this all over the country—from neighborhoods to the White House—and I am good at it. But the reason I have done that is because I believe in something much bigger than just the act of choosing a school. I believe that the unique character of every person is needed as a contribution to who we are as a whole. This shared society can't afford to cast anybody off, or make them less than they were meant to be. In our society, in this country, we absolutely need the best of everything that everyone has to offer.

That belief has driven me to spend much of my lifetime confronting laws about how and where and why we create schools. Right now, the education system robs children of their phenomenal potential. I do not mean intentionally, but I do mean *systematically*. And that is a fact.

So hoping to grow the number of those committed to getting this right, I wanted to write about *why* I do my work rather than *how* I do it. I am not going to say much more about the how in this book. But do know that I believe with all my heart that school choice is one among all the very serious choices that shape children for their role in society, and insisting on it will improve every community in this country—and in turn perhaps, the world.

Why I do that work is a function of who I was made to be, the experiences and environments my parents chose for me, and then gradually, what I came to believe about this life we all share. I have traveled plenty of roads that are common to many of us, but too often make our life or our children's lives sadder rather than happier. I was taught to arrive at being happier by staying focused on larger purposes. My parents taught all of their children that although we were special, we were special for a *purpose*. Just being happy wasn't something to seek… happy is a byproduct of steering toward other, more essential things. That orientation was a huge gift, and I hope their teaching—which became my ability to navigate—can help others to choose environments that result in happier lives for both children and adults.

Finally, I believe with all my heart and soul that everyone is sent here to earth to be of service. We are here for each other, and we are all we've got. So we have to get good at that. We have to be the best us we can be, and help children to do the same. I am blessed with a family that embodies that belief, and I've chosen to share them simply as one great example of getting this orientation right.

In telling my stories, I hope to share an addiction to the joy that life makes available to all of us. While the book offers life advice, I seek to avoid brutal directives and focus instead on what is possible and what can be fun. Because I am known to be a professional-grade expert in silly fun.

Thank you, reader, for picking up this book and learning what I have to say. Writing this book has been an absolute privilege.

Chapter One

A Chosen Path

*P*art of my deep expertise in silly fun arose from my first career, and the boss who became my best friend, life sounding board, editor of all things typed and another mother to my children. I studied linguistics at Stanford—best to college name-drop this from the start lest you think I learned all these really nifty things on the street—and then received my master's degree in communication disorders from Arizona State University. Having been overeducated by age 22, I interned as a speech pathologist specializing in neurological damage at the Phoenix Veteran's Administration Health Care System during the last year of my master's degree. That was a big deal, and it was the gift of a lifetime.

My boss and mentor Pat Holtzapple (later Weinberg) was one of the best clinicians in the country—duly noted as such by her colleagues—and the source of the most intensely personal therapeutic technique I have ever encountered. Pat believed that you couldn't treat somebody you didn't know, and that unless you understood more about people than the contours of their brain scans, you would likely make little progress together. Working with Pat was intense, demanding, and the best life training in personal communication imaginable.

Emerging from this career with a specialty in neurological damage was a plus. Years later, as I attended lunches where I was introduced as a potential candidate for the state legislature, former Arizona congressman Sam Steiger told me that my background in brain damage made me the world's first truly qualified political candidate. It is not generous for me to comment on how right Sam was.

My career experience with hospitalized veterans was far more than clinical. My life was made immeasurably richer by the people I was privileged to meet. In 1982, most of the patients we worked with were World War II veterans in the prime risk years for stroke—and many had suffered one. And although I regretted the reason they were there, their presence in the hospital offered an incredible lesson in courage for me. First of all, these guys were tough. Not just about their condition, although they were that indeed. But they had mastered courage long before a stroke compromised their speech. I had the incredible privilege of listening to the stories of their war service as part of our work together. And because group discussion was often their most productive—if still frustrating—communication of the week, we had many such discussions. The guys were much more interested in hearing each other and each other's stories than in talking for the sake of it.

There is no way to explain what these men were to each other and to all of us without listening to them talk firsthand. They changed the world for us, and they knew it. But they knew they had changed the world together, by virtue of a shared commitment. It wasn't something they paraded; it was something they were.

In my political world, we hear the word "brave" tossed around a lot. We say about people who run for office that they are "brave" to take the onslaught of nastiness that attends campaigning. We are told that standing up for one's beliefs in the face of political opposition is "brave." I don't think so. I prefer to think that standing up to the public honestly should be the least we can expect from elected representatives.

Working at the VA hospital, I saw "brave." Yes, I saw real, honest-to-God *brave* in the faces of dozens of men who had not necessarily been overtly heroic. But they had placed themselves in harm's way for a belief in their mission and a belief in the guy next to them. And then, having worked through the horror of war to win the world some peace in that era, they lived lives of quiet acceptance—until life assaulted them yet again. And they fought back from that for their families, for themselves, and because of the VA environment, they fought with their friends again. It was a uniquely rich opportunity for them as well as me, and one I don't ever take for granted.

So I told you that I learned silly fun at the VA. That may seem odd, given the intense and life-altering damage these veterans had sustained.

Well, as it turns out, military service during wartime—walking side by side with death— can instill a sense of comedy. I suspect it is because the veterans became hauntingly familiar with their own mortality, and worried less over the small details of themselves and the world around them. Instead, they learned to embrace the potential for happiness or inspiration that any given moment has to offer. The veterans I worked with had walked that precarious walk early in their lives, they valued a happy life, and they carried that like contagion.

I suspect that those who work in other hospitals experience a version of this same thing. The fear and pain that accompany illness, combined with the intensity of hope and roller-coaster emotions, give rise to a particular brand of dark humor that keeps everybody going.

In the combination of war veterans with the traditional hospital humor cocktail, I found myself embracing life right out loud. As I write this, I am *actively* editing most of the funniest stories from those days because they are simply wrong when read out of context. At a minimum, they are offensive. But at their best and most offensive, the memory of our shared laughter still lifts my heart.

The language around the hospital was crude to begin with— something unnecessary to explain to the military folks who are reading this. But a common fact of brain injury is that the coarsest, most obscene expressions of language will remain intact even when the milder and more socially acceptable dulcet tones of discourse have been obliterated. In other words, we all swore a lot and it was because often, that's all we could do.

Simple Choices

I remember the first time Pat explained to me this phenomenon of expletive persistence in the face of no other speech. I had read about it, but as an art form, it must be experienced. Imagine being a young, eager, 22 year-old success junkie, manners honed to debutante perfection, sitting in a room with a decorated army veteran. And together, we are belting out the classics: "Shit! Fuck! Bullshit! Mother-Fucker!" Very little in the classical liberal arts education prepares one for this.

We had depth in our therapeutic repertoire as well, and Pat was also an expert in melodic intonation therapies. Often music or melody could assist in recovering words for one whose speech was compromised. The theory proposed improvement by engaging the unimpaired right side of the brain, thus treatment consisted of simple three or four word phrases sung out to a simple melody. For example, we'd sing the three syllables of "Hello, Fred" laid over the tones of "Three Blind Mice" while tapping each beat on the table.

Pat was always better at melodic intonation than I was until I discovered that one of my patients could combine expletives with melodies and create a pretty raucous—and *fluent*—ditty that it turns out everybody on the next ward over wanted to learn! The nurses loved us.

Hey, we were in the business of communicating essentials. You would be amazed what can be expressed with only the four basic lewd groups.

Because it is a true classic, I will share that ditty and explain why it is far more than silly or obscene. Take the tune of *Frère Jacques (Are You Sleeping?)* and substitute those first words with "Mo-ther Fuck-er", then repeat. Second line substitution for *Dormez-Vous?* (*Brother John*) is "Hey, Fuck You!", also repeated. I know, it's beautiful. When it's put altogether, the singer may gustily offer:

"Moth-er Fuck-er, Moth-er Fuck-er...Hey, Fuck You! Hey, Fuck You!"

The reason to reach for something this outrageous is that dignity is preserved in communication. Any communication. Imagine the embarrassment that attends being unable to communicate even the most basic of greetings, needs, or ideas. It is a horrifying predicament that is wholly blameless for its victim, but it diminishes the spirit and induces shame nonetheless. Swearing, on the other hand, is the domain of the confident. Or of the aggressive. Regardless, it is not associated with the meek or those to be pitied. Regaining the opportunity for spirited dialogue - even if offensive -reconnected our veterans to who they had been. Much better to successfully hail somebody with a hardy "Hey, Fuck You!" than a silent and failed struggle to produce "How are you?" Rest assured that "Hey, Fuck You!" was quickly edited back to a simple "Hey!" after confidence was recovered. Far more than words alone, we worked to reclaim the spirit.

I don't want to make it sound as though swearing is all we VA speech pathologists did. We just did it well when we had to. The totality of the work was intense, and it was difficult. For us, certainly, but mostly for the families whose relationship with their spouses or parents was now compromised due to an inability to share the daily information that families rely on.

This work at the VA taught me what true service looks like, and it also focused my perspective in two very profound ways.

First, I developed an absolute awe for the power of the brain and its ability to dictate the terms by which humans display their essence. And I understood its ability to offer us far more than we usually ask. I saw miracles in the face of physical devastation, and I saw potential squandered for lack of effort or expectation. It became very clear to me that personal effort determined success – that was not a news bulletin. More powerful by far was observing the degree to which the *willingness* to exert or risk oneself was inspired or diminished by the behavior and beliefs of others. Time and again, I observed the effects of friends, family, and therapists as they cast either lights or shadows on our patients' struggles to progress. While I absolutely believe that individuals control their own behaviors, I gained the humbling understanding that my actions and expectations could inspire or discourage another's will, their effort, and thus their ultimate chance to succeed.

This interplay of personal effort enmeshed with the constant encouragement and positive expectation of those around us cannot be ignored. People affect each other deeply. We rely on each other's expectation of our best effort. And though it seems out of fashion to admit this belief, I became convinced that not only must we offer our own best efforts; we owe those around us our expectation that they, too, will offer their best.

The second major gift the work at the VA gave me was a solidified love for communication. The ability to speak to one another, or to attempt to understand one another, is fraught with difficulty in the best of circumstances. But striving to do that well, to share thoughts and to comprehend the life of another? That is magic. Language can decorate the world, support people who are struggling, inspire folks to action and increase understanding. It is a brush in an artist's hands, a strategic weapon when called upon and a means to creating relationships.

I'm a big believer in the power of words, and I am grateful for them. I believe in writing things down, and in talking it out up close and personal. And in swearing when you have to, obviously.

My work at the VA lasted about five years. I loved the work, and I fell in love with Pat as everybody who ever met her did. So Pat and I stayed together, but the VA and I parted ways.

I left for a number of reasons. I had the opportunity to lead a grant project at Arizona State University, but there also was the fact that tightly defined systems like the VA and I didn't mesh well. I was focused on solving patient issues, and the VA needed for me to be a bit more focused on things that made absolutely no sense to me. I was beginning to appreciate that having freedom of choice, and freedom to create new solutions was going to be a hallmark of my personality. That was not so positive to the man saddled with supervising me. I worked for Pat, but she reported to somebody else, and he was a quintessential rule guy. To be fair, that was the VA way, and he was good at it.

When I left the VA, Pat's supervisor wrote out a lovely and clever medical discharge summary for me with the diagnosis "Unsuccessful Bureaucratic Conversion." Then he toasted me at the going-away party by commenting on my consistent march to a different drummer. Pat and I sensed it was not intended as flattery, and I still have the drummer boy figurine Pat gave me to herald the moment.

So I left the VA, and worked with ASU for just about a year before I had to contend with my growing sense that I should be trying to create change in a different sphere.

I followed that sense into the state legislature after my former husband and I joked about drawing straws to decide which one of us should run for office, since obviously somebody had to do it. In 1989, Arizona was in the midst of one of our political moments. Arizona has lots of these; we may not beat out other states, but we are a colorful contender. Shortly after the gubernatorial election of 1988, it became increasingly obvious that Governor Evan Mecham was, um, problematic for the job. But more graphic even than his bizarre antics and frequently offensive commentary was the opportunity to watch our state elected officials in action. Mecham had so offended the legislators that they began impeachment hearings…all of which were televised.

I don't know if the legislators thought that would be a good thing for them or not, but for me, it was like watching a train wreck. I tend toward the overly optimistic in my assessments of people and institutions; a person will have to try pretty hard to insult me with their behavior. In this case, I was insulted without anybody making an effort. No doubt these were basically good people, but the moment was not stellar for many of them.

So I thought my voice could add a needed dimension on behalf of the community and I ran for the Arizona House in 1990. And I won. Thus began my next career path, and a whole new set of ways to have silly fun.

But as with most things, the process was not what I thought it would be. I came to the Arizona legislature with a warped view of what community leadership would look like. For one thing, I had just recently completed my participation in Valley Leadership, which is something that I highly recommend to you, as most communities offer this kind of leadership training. It's an opportunity to meet with others who wish to serve their communities, and to learn about the various sectors of business and government. And it's high-level, best-case scenario stuff. You meet the folks involved in these sectors who volunteer to participate because they also have an optimistic view of the workings of the community.

Thus, I entered this phase of my life with warped expectations.

Plus, I had taken on leadership positions in my community as the volunteer president of the YWCA, where we were working on transitional housing for women and children who were fleeing domestic violence situations. I was also on the board of directors for Planned Parenthood.

I should pause here so you can process how I spent my life in Republican politics, won every election I entered (I'm amazing, really) and started that whole process while holding a position of leadership at the local Planned Parenthood.

What? Well, there are lots of good explanations for that.

First of all, as I believe I may have mentioned in the title of this book and on every page since, I am obsessed with allowing people to be who they are by insisting on their free choices. So it is important to me to be consistent about that.

Second, although you don't hear all of us as loudly and clearly as you should, there are *lots* of Republicans who believe that government truly should not play a role in any area of civic life that is better left to the individual. In fact, my favorite leaders on this issue are bra-carrying Republicans. I feel strongly about this and fear that it is one of several issues where we have worn away the prerogative of our churches by confusing government and church roles in our lives. Decisions about bringing children into the world are so intimate and so intensely spiritual;

nobody outside those immediately affected and their trusted confidants can possibly understand or counsel well.

I accept that a good number of the people reading this book may very well stop reading it right now because of my beliefs on this issue. And I get that. Having to deal with this intensity very early on in my political career taught me deep respect for those who engage in honest disagreement over any issues. The experience surely taught me how to navigate the passions surrounding school choice.

The strength of my own commitment makes me quite aware of how strongly those around me feel, so I don't think less of people solely because we disagree. This is just part of life's complexity... truly wonderful people disagree about the most basic of issues. We are different; we all see the world differently. In my humble and somewhat mystic opinion, we are made to see the world differently so that we can balance each other. Our shared responsibility is to find a way to create a society that accommodates all of us. Having an assortment of friends and acquaintances whose opinions run the gamut on life's controversial issues hopefully reflects a healthy, open mind. I know it makes life far more interesting!

So. If you're still with me, the final reason for my involvement in Planned Parenthood is that my great-grandmother Margaret Hitchcock Doorly (lovingly Nona) was a supporter of its founder, Margaret Sanger, and encouraged her work. Years later, my grandmother (Nona's daughter) Katherine Doorly (Young) Clark sat on the local board of Planned Parenthood in Omaha, and our family has had a woman in every generation since serve on a local board. I feel strongly about families building on the positive contributions of their ancestors.

The initial rationale for my family's involvement with family planning did not have anything to do with the more controversial issues of today...it had to do with the controversial issues of those days. You will remember that in the late 1800s, congress passed the Comstock Act, which made it illegal to disseminate contraception or information about controlling fertility. It was considered obscenity. At that same time, my family was in the newspaper business in Omaha. We owned the *Omaha World-Herald* and Nona was committed to making the facts on fertility and contraception available. My great-grandmother was no rabble-rouser, but she did believe in the power of information. And since our family was in a position to provide that via the newspaper and an ongoing role in Nebraska's state and national political leadership, her interest alone was powerful.

This period of history was important for my side of the family—and for my husband's family too. At nearly the exact same time my family was navigating this issue and many others in Nebraska, my husband's great-grandfather J.J. Keegan was a member of Arizona's constitutional convention. Arizona statehood also became a high water mark for the progress of women's rights. Members of the territory's convention tried to include the right for women to vote as part of their new constitution when they submitted it in late 1911, but President Taft was having none of it. The suffrage movement was working its way across the country, and he felt that the issue was not ripe for conclusion. In other words, this wasn't his thing.

No matter, the Arizona contingent relented, but they had included in the constitution some new provisions for referendum and initiative, hallmarks of the populist American West. After statehood was granted to Arizona on Valentine's Day of 1912, the legislature put women's suffrage on the ballot, and women gained the vote in November of that year via a significant majority of (male!) votes. That's right, Arizona and a few other Western states beat the rest of you guys—well, gals—by about seven years.

My husband and I are products of families with a tradition of support for women and family issues, which was one but one aspect of their broader work to offer leadership in their communities. Even more essentially, our families believed deeply in the power of information and the rights of the public to *act* according to personal principle. We are both proud of that legacy and grateful for the opportunity to follow their examples.

So I attribute my brand of politics to family history. I'm a woman who likes choice in the marketplace and I like it at home. Because of this strong stake in having freedom of choice, I don't fit in with any single brand, party or belief when it comes to politics. This, too, is consistent with family history. My great-great grandfather, Gilbert Hitchcock (Margaret Doorly's father and founder of the *Omaha World-Herald*), was both a U.S. representative and U.S. senator as a Democrat from Nebraska, after his father Phineas set the example by holding those same offices as a Republican. Gilbert had been persuaded to change his party affiliation over concerns for agricultural issues specific to Nebraska and by his early admiration for William Jennings Bryan.

At the time Gilbert decided to switch parties, he had just married Jessie Crounse Hitchcock, daughter of the former Republican congressman and future governor, Lorenzo Crounse. Oops. I suspect that made their Thanksgiving gatherings a bit awkward for a while, but I also know there was an abiding affection between the two.

My husband, John Keegan, had to navigate this same partisan divide when he first ran for Arizona's state legislature. The Keegans have been active in Arizona politics since territorial days, and in those early days as consistent Democrats, the majority party at the time of statehood. When John ran for his first political office, his grandmother called to say how pleased she was to read an article about him in the paper. But she wanted him to know her friends had pointed out a terrible misprint—the article suggested he was a Republican. John was busted and had to share his truth with her. This was followed by a palpable and icy silence, broken by this predictable inquiry: "Does your father know?" Ah, family. Sometimes you disappoint them even while you're making them proud.

It always seemed to me in reading their histories that my grandfathers saw their political parties as tools for advancing particular

11

philosophies rather than as entities to be supported for their own sakes. I am a happy practitioner of the same perspective.

Well, as it happens in the current moment, I am an often unhappy practitioner of party politics as I think my own party has navigated against its core principles. But because I most strongly identify with the foundational Republican beliefs in freedom and individual initiative over centrally imposed restraints, I simply assume we have a lot of work to do.

A lot of work.

Wanting to be hopeful is in my genes. Regardless of which party the politicians in my family have represented over the years, the consistent theme in their leadership roles has been to address the future with committed optimism. One of many lessons we heard as children was the story of Gilbert Hitchcock's role in leading the U.S. Senate battle for creation of a League of Nations on behalf of President Woodrow Wilson.

Since I am aware that U.S. history is not an educational strength for Americans, you are forgiven if you do not remember how this went. I fear I would have no insights about it myself were it not personal. At the end of World War I there was surge of democratic rule around the world, with elected leaders replacing warring despots. Many believed that the war's end had created the promise for a lasting peace among nations. The League of Nations was proposed as a means to this end, through enforced and ongoing dialogue among the world's leaders. The speech Gilbert gave on the Senate floor to inspire his colleagues toward a vote for the League has a prominent position in our family scrapbook, and we recently discovered a website with a genuine recording of that 1918 speech. God bless the Internet. That website is www.authentichistory.com, and it is an amazing archive.

Here are some of Gilbert's words which are so poignant, and an exhortation to his colleagues to seize on a unique and potent moment in history:

"Let them appreciate the fact that humanity is not willing to sacrifice itself further, that men and women demand of their government

that as a fruit of this terrible war an agreement shall be entered into for the preservation of world peace in the future."

He had such hope. It's easy to look back in hindsight and know this was not to be, but difficult to hold my family's perspective that includes an abiding sense of loss. What if the U.S. Congress and the world community had adopted a more expansive and hopeful view? Gilbert was one of many who believed that combining the harsh terms of the Treaty of Versailles with an absence of ongoing formal dialogue among world leaders had inextricably laid the groundwork for another war. He was right about the thing he least wanted to be right about.

A particularly difficult aspect of this defeat was that when President Wilson went to Versailles to negotiate the treaty, and to exhort his colleagues in France and Great Britain to refrain from attempting to humiliate Germany, he did so with a small cadre of advisors that included not a single Republican. And Wilson did that because he was angry at Republicans who refused to support his efforts to create and join a League of Nations. In an act steeped in irony - his anger at his colleagues' unwillingness to see the possibilities for peace through ongoing communication - he chose to humiliate these fellow Americans rather than continue to include them in a negotiation process. That act did not help the League's future.

Politics is a deeply human, and therefore often deeply flawed exercise.

And that is true regardless of the party you join, the issues you support, or the relationships you nurture with colleagues or opponents along the way. Nothing is simple, everything is complex, and the world really needs for all of us to be both well informed and humble when taking on the very difficult task of trying to shape a better future. But flawed human nature that begets flawed political process does not negate perfect intent; it is always right to try.

The inherent complexity of life is why I believe our nation's greatest hope is ensuring that every child has access to an outstanding education. Excellent education is essential to the individual's ability to choose a meaningful life path, to be certain. But for all of us to continue our journey as a healthy democracy - to ensure that the precious yet historically precarious ideals of a democratic republic can endure - education is our best chance.

My own understanding of the best leaders our country has known is that they possessed both wisdom and humility. They were not without ego, but they were secure and learned. History does give us examples of those without much formal education that buck the odds and become great leaders, but frankly not many. What great leaders know…is that they don't always know. And that kind of wisdom comes from learning enough to be humbled by the enormity and complexity of the world we share. Great leaders know this, and so they rely on informing their insight with the wisdom of others; great leaders invite a vigorous exchange of ideas. It takes a great deal of intellectual confidence to follow a path that invites debate, and never moreso than when one is in a position of power. But that has been the genius of our democracy. The more we have sought the highest ideal, the greatest inclusion, the most difficult debates—the stronger we have become. As we disregard debate and avoid complexity in favor of simplistic bromides, we risk the future.

There just is no simplicity, no single side one can always root for. We must always acknowledge the strengths and the weaknesses of our ideas and our actions.

As an easy example, let's consider the issue of family planning, because I consider that topic a family victory of sorts. Positive as it is for me, history tends to put a simplistic happy gloss over big events. If you know this story well, you will know that not all aspects of the efforts to provide women information about fertility were savory. There was without question a strong current of opinion that wanted birth control to be "applied" to low income families, as a means of shaping the populace. I think that the term "unsavory" is a generous descriptor of that intention. That reality, however, sits alongside the fact that the family planning/

female contraception movement did give women the information and control they needed over their lives and their families.

The moral complexity that attends issues such as this has fascinated me for all of my life. Excellent causes are often advanced in part to carry along less idealistic projects or interests. Or they are only advanced by the use of less than idealistic strategies. No single issue or single organization is ethically sound in all quarters or even strategically consistent. Yet *awareness of moral complexity* is not daunting; and acknowledging it need not weaken one's resolve for improvement. There will ultimately be a way forward that most will agree can serve the highest and best good.

As a small example in the case of Planned Parenthood, I have remained aligned with their major issues all of my adult life. But when I ran for state school superintendent in Arizona after two terms in the Arizona House of Representatives, they would not endorse me because of my stand in support of school choice. So I called a friend on the Planned Parenthood board to…um…inquire about this. I was told that the director had determined that people who supported school choice were also religious fundamentalists who opposed Planned Parenthood.

Hmmm… obviously not. I reminded him that I supported choice in both realms, but I did not make any headway with the organization and had to battle through a statewide election, in a Republican state, as a Republican, and without the key support of a family planning organization. I'm being facetious. Planned Parenthood probably did me a favor because I won the office decisively. But the facts of the experience were instructive.

For me, the fight for freedom of choice in realms where choice is limited is a first order issue. So I don't change my mind about the idea just because lots of friends change their minds about me. Plus, there is an element of truth in their concern. Many of the people who fight very hard for choice in schooling oppose choices for women when it comes to their healthcare. You can't be an honest advocate without accepting that your battle for one thing may very well advance another that you oppose. Even if you have disciplined your mind to create some of the world's coolest smarty-pants ideas, it's best to get comfortable with humility.

To take on the role of leader and advocate, an individual must be aware of what he or she could cause to happen just in case luck joins intention and leads to success. Remember, even the greatest, most morally sound decisions of all time carried little ethically challenged hitch-hikers. You have to introduce yourself to the intentions of the people who will both ride and resist your bandwagon and manage them, or else you end up working very hard on things that will ultimately have shallow value or worse.

It is usually true that opponents of your idea aren't so much ethically challenged as they are advocates of a bunch of things you don't like. Sometimes they actually improve the quality of your idea, and you will need to invite them on board. It is quite difficult to acknowledge that no idea you offer into the public discourse will remain as beautiful and pristine as that same idea sitting daintily cosseted inside your head. I have learned over the years to wrap my pure and dainty ideas in sturdier garments offered by others. They end up less aesthetically pure…less pleasing to those whose tastes in idealistic art mirror mine…but they live longer. Durable solutions are rarely dainty; they're kind of a bulky mess, really. And it takes a fair amount of calm and confidence to let your pretty little idea take on this added bulk and unwieldy aspect. It's all so much lovelier when it's just you and your idea alone.

Advocates for any issue have an obligation to be informed, persuasive and clear in all communications about their pursuit. In my case, I can draw my vision of a utopian education system on a napkin. And that simple illustrated definition is based on understanding the history of American education, the complex theories of contemporary thinkers, plus the foundational wisdom of some stellar dead men and women, including Friedrich von Hayek and Milton and Rose Friedman.

My visions and ideas took long hours and a diligent intellectual search to develop. The humility I didn't have to go looking for; possessing a willingness to share my ideas and to try to enshrine them into law or into the hearts of others has caused humility to come hurling at me.

Which brings me all the way back to why I wrote this book before writing about the issues I champion. I am compelled by a belief that all of us owe the community, country and world we live in our very best service. I did not come up with that idea by myself—it has been the topic of family dinner conversation since long before my husband or I was born. What I heard growing up was not specifically what I should think or believe, although let's face it, there were some very specific hopes.

More importantly, what I heard was that my family expected me to work very hard to become somebody who could contribute something of value. Not just opinions, but work, support and understanding on behalf of others. Nowhere are those efforts more critical than when we make them on behalf of our children. And nowhere is it more difficult to set aside what I might want in favor of risking a reality less under my personal control. But I recognize that the thing I don't control may be destined to serve a purpose far greater than I had contemplated.

For me, the responsibilities toward family, friends and society are quite similar. My public work is akin to mothering a whole host of burgeoning thinkers…not trying to control what they contribute…just wanting to make sure they can be heard. And that is the work of raising the next generation. Everyone influences the future by giving those who follow us the capacity to contribute their own service, according to their own talents, and toward the betterment of the world we share.

And I learned this from my family. For us, great decisions for children revolve around developing an ability to be fully informed, and then selecting the best of all the imperfect options available. It's a matter of having and making simple choices.

Chapter Two

Choosing Motherhood

*T*he happiest choice I ever made was to be a mother.

Well, actually, this was a combination of my choice, my former husband's choice and some divine intervention. Regardless, it's been indescribable joy…and surprising as hell.

I was 29 years old when my first child finally showed up…after nine months of excruciatingly correct pregnancy behavior on my part and a belief that I could manage the labor thing everybody else complained about with the grace befitting my mother's daughter. That's a high bar.

The belief provided me with what I deserved…an incredible opportunity to be humbled. After 20 hours into labor unaided by painkillers (I have a need to be admired for my fortitude) I was rolled into an operating room where a combination of power tools and vacuums couldn't match the effectiveness of the largest nurse I have ever seen literally climbing on a chair so she could better access my abdomen… adding the full force of her considerable being to my efforts. It wasn't elegant.

But all that action brought me my baby, and I contend to this day it was a natural childbirth.

Despite the flourish accompanying his arrival, the most forceful realization of the moment had nothing to do with delivery. It was recognizing a completely independent soul in the eyes of my son Justin.

I remember looking into his eyes and being shocked at his independence. He was all of eight pounds, he had literally been connected to me until just that moment for all of his life, and I imagined that I would feel that he was a part of me.

I didn't.

I recognized a fellow traveler. Where I had thought I would see a part of me, or a part of me and his father; I saw a new part of *us*...big *us*, community *us*, as in all of *us*. It's a sense that has never waned, and it represented a welcome shift in my expectation. I immediately understood that my role was as partner—albeit senior partner when he was little—and, as somebody who was to prepare this person for a life whose purpose would never truly be understood by me. I was tasked with preparation, not implementation. Justin's life was to be his own, and it had already been shaped and planned for by the Big Partner, as mine had been. It was a shattering realization; it broke my heart in two immediately because I now knew that I couldn't...I wouldn't...protect him from a world I knew would hurt him.

But I also gained a peace in that moment that I have never lost. Everything my own mother had told me about *purpose* for all of my life, I finally understood. Parents don't bestow it on children, they nurture it. Children come fully equipped.

It is this overwhelming responsibility to provide everything necessary for a child to become who they were meant to be that has obsessed me for my entire adult life. I wish I had felt that kind of certainty more often in my life. I could have been struck by so many of these moments, been so full of universal recognitions, that I could have become a sage in a robe on a hill somewhere. I think I could have excelled as a sage, a dispenser of wisdom, up on a hill.

That's not what happened. After more than fifty years, I know without reservation that the one and only grand plan for me—the thing my mother could not know when she first looked in my eyes—was to be hit with just this single realization that became a life's obsession: Children are capable of the most phenomenal things. All of them. Regardless of what we planned for, expected or designed, they arrive here with everything they need to contribute themselves to bettering the world we share, in a way completely unique to them. Beyond loving them unreservedly, our job as their parents/community…no small task, incidentally…is to seek out and provide the environments which will inspire and cultivate the very best our children have to offer.

Let me admit the obvious. Believing that you are living according to a divinely inspired plan reflects a great amount of confidence. And I often wonder when I proclaim my faith in a purposeful plan if the savior I report to isn't leaning over to an angel assistant to inquire, "Hmmm… hearing from a Lisa Keegan today…says she knows us… check her membership status and get back to me."

I realize for many of my friends, my quiet faith seems to indicate only light duty in the Christian community. As a possible explanation/ excuse for any apparent lack of fervor, I offer the fact that I belong to a longstanding tradition of Episcopalian practice, where proper attire and a hushed practice of faith are both considered essential. Our family is, indeed, a happy band of God's frozen chosen.

So my traditions and my comforts both lie in an immutable and private faith. It can be difficult for outsiders to discern, but I think it's what we Episcopalians strive to attain. I am deeply grateful for and humbled by my faith.

And my belief in a life's purpose that is divinely inspired is not a gift I think is unique to me. I think it's unique to all of us—completely unique, as any relationship is. It has always been easy for me to accept different faiths among my friends and neighbors, as my parents were clear that the God who calls to you is calling you on pretty intimate terms. It is not for you to decide how He calls to others. Your relationship with God is your unique relationship; your duties to that relationship are yours, and they will be sufficient for your energies. There is no need for you to dictate terms for the spiritual lives of others...just try to live the example you think is being asked of you. It's enough. It's usually far more than enough.

When I was growing up, my parents made it very clear to us that we were subject to what was being asked of us. We were expected to make a difference; we were expected to find our purpose. They never suggested that our path was somehow going to be superior to anybody else's and they never suggested they knew what our path would be. They simply knew we had a purpose; it was our job to discover what we could do to improve the world. That message wasn't presented as a burden, and it certainly never felt that way. It was just a fact of our family. It is our story.

My parents, my aunts, uncles, and grandparents were obsessive about introducing us to the family, those on this plane and to the memory of those who had already crossed over. They sought out good examples for us in the family history, and much of that story was ever so subtly grounded in faith. Except in the case of my father Richard Fletcher, who has always claimed that he is agnostic...a fact that constantly confirms for me the mysteries of a life based on faith versus living one's life with no claimed faith. The assets of faith certainly claimed my dad, as there is no better man. My own faith tells me that this agnostic father I love was always meant for me, even though he didn't belong to me until he adopted me when I was three years old.

So my story has always had faith in a grand plan and a Grand Planner as its background, but playing softly. We aren't ones to wake the neighbors with religious proclamation. My grandmother (mom's mother, Bami) in particular disdained public displays of religiosity. She liked the front row of the church, but only because everybody *in* the church already wanted to be there; she believed that there is a time and a place for everything. Bami was a serious figure in our family, who believed wholeheartedly that decorum mattered. Not so much for its own sake, but because we belonged to a long history of family members who had dedicated themselves to the betterment of their community—which would become our community—and she reminded us frequently that their legacy was our privilege and our responsibility.

The business of storytelling and event marking as inspirations to each other is a discipline in our family, as serious as any job or commitment we make. Writing the family story is an ongoing, happy obligation. As children, we were fed a regular diet of family biography. We heard the personal stories at a steady stream of family events; my mother and her sisters wrote songs at each of these events that we were all obliged to sing for my grandparents; we received little printed quotations that some family member loved; we could expect cards written by family members marking events or recalling a family member's story; we read scrapbooks full of family news clippings or personal letters that reflected our ancestors' hopes and dreams; we received small handmade books about family members who had passed over. And we all received scrapbooks in order to house our own life's personal merit badges along the way.

Spending time together has always been essential—it defines our family. Like many families, we kind of picked a dominant side which was my mother's—the distaff side. I am sure the fact that my father and uncles had lovingly bestowed my grandmother Bami with the nickname "Nails" (as in pounded, not polished) had something to do with that seemingly free choice. My mother, Daphne Young Fletcher, is one of four sisters, and we grew up right next door to my Aunt Susie Young Charlton and her family in Phoenix. Susie was mom's younger sister. My mother's twin, Diane Young Hamsa, lived right next door to their older sister Gail Young Koch in Omaha, and though we lived in two different states, all of us gathered for family events at least once or twice a year.

One of our gathering places was my mother's former winter home in Palm Springs, California called Smoke Tree Ranch. We didn't just drop by now and then…this was a permanent installment of three houses that could accommodate 25 people. Twice a year. My grandparents had their house, and then bought two more houses so that the four girls and their families could share them. We were in Palm Springs often enough and for long enough that there was an actual little schoolhouse we had to attend to complete schoolwork we were missing at home.

I have numerous family photos spanning those years, showing all 14 cousins dressed for dinner at the Ranch House…and we matched. Seriously, special occasions would mean matching dinner dresses that coordinated with our brothers' matching suits. Dinner might be a a hayride to a steak cookout where we would sing along with a local cowboy Johnny Boyle…potentially wearing matching cowboy hats. I still know the words to "Tumbling Tumbleweeds."

Goofiness aside, it was pretty heavenly. We had amazing adventures with each other and a pretty free run of the place. The ranch was a secluded neighborhood with plenty of opportunity for everything kids could want to do. And since my grandparents lived there half the year, everybody knew we were Bami and Pop's grandkids and lack of anonymity was its own enforcer. None of us wanted to face off with Bami.

These Smoke Tree stays were in addition to overseas adventures my grandparents took us all on, adding my grandfather's side of the family and a few nannies so they could all escape us for dinner occasionally. But when we did eat together for special occasions, the younger children, of which I was one, wore coordinated outfits. I think my grandmother must have loved that, and possibly requested/demanded it…who knew the difference?

Plus, being the children of twins you grow up understanding there is some weird permanent connection between the twin moms and you just end up being in sync even when you didn't plan it. So we got to tour Europe on two separate occasions with our band of two dozen plus, emerging every so often from our hotel rooms looking frighteningly similar to the Von Trapp Family. At every one of these family occasions there was a mandatory evening performance and sing-a-long, resulting in photography that provides all of the cousins both happy memories and occasional ammunition for current day family dinners.

In summers, the twin sisters spent time together at Ten Mile Lake in northern Minnesota, which meant more togetherness for the cousins, as several of our non-twin cousins would join from time to time. Happily, that practice continues to this day as Ten Mile now houses five separate family houses with another cousin at a next door lake. I get my best writing done up at the lake and as I was recently memorializing in writing this phenomenon of matching outfits, I noticed a picture taken up here of the five girls back in the day: me, my sister and our cousins. We would have been about high school age in this picture, seemingly beyond the matching outfit stage. But no, there we are…sitting together on the dock stairs…in matching t-shirts decorated with frogs.

When confronted with this section of my book, my mother took great umbrage, declaring "That cannot be true. We had better things to do than run around shopping for matching outfits for you all."

Well, apparently not. I confirmed the family fashion folly with numerous cousins and abundant photos. And we seem to be in accord that the apex of this habit came at my grandfather Pop's 80th birthday party in Palm Springs, where purple gingham was the order of the day. Lots of it.

I wonder if this slightly creepy habit simply measures my family's devotion to creating team spirit? Whatever it was, it worked. We cousins still seek each other out, and our own children have grown up with these summers and have become very close, something I am sure my grandmother is orchestrating from on high…although she has not managed to impose a matching dress code from up there. I have met my children and I can't see that ever happening. She will have to content herself with knowing that the children all know, love and support each other, even if they don't match.

I grew to understand that writing the family narrative was not to be taken lightly. While it seemed to be mostly a lot of fun...it was more than that. It established family as foundation, it made us who we are, or confirmed who we are, and committed us to a principle of community.

It has always been abundantly clear to me that my story is nothing less—and nothing more—than a next chapter in an already wonderful book. No single one of us is the beginning or end of our family story. But the story has a rhythm, its plot is already established, it is a good story. It wants to go on being told. Living as one of many, many protagonists in an age-old, happy and well-read history is a very secure place to be. Extremely secure.

And I highly recommend it. Not necessarily the full-on Bami approach that requires my grandmother's means and commitment. No, but the ritual of it, the constant getting together and creating stories, poems and music about family adventures. It is the business of setting a family's character and purpose in stone...developing the ability to see ourselves and still love ourselves...over time and in all circumstance. Obviously at every gathering there were—and are still—a few moments of high drama; 25 people getting along is a lot to expect. But it is a grace of our family to seek the humor in every situation, and whatever big dramas occurred during our get-together would likely reappear as comedy schtick in the end-of-vacation poem or song. And the message was not subtle: "We see you for who you are, and we love you because of it...or maybe anyway. But you belong to us and we expect you to add important chapters to this *Book of Us*."

Only as I got older did I realize that this kind of security-inducing ritual was not universal practice for every family. Nor could I have understood the degree to which this disciplined creation of a family's story had established expectations for the way I live my life and guide my children's lives that nothing else could have created.

I expect that my children and the children whose lives I affect will seek to be everything they were meant to be. I expect them to matter a great deal to the world, just as I expect everybody to matter a great deal to the world. Children come with gifts, talents and trajectories unique to themselves, and the poetry of life is that if you can successfully enable your child to access those things, they get to make a difference to everybody around them. They get to continue writing the story—yours and theirs.

Pretty sweet.

Chapter Three

Choice and Expectation

*E*xpecting the best of children is not about every child becoming a uniform and perfect member of the world community. If there is one thing that growing up in big families teaches, it is that everybody's an original. Sometimes *very* original. Plus, I'm not a big fan of uniform and perfect. I like originality, and I think the world depends on it.

In fact, I think the one sure way to live the unhappy life is to decide exactly what your life and your childrens' lives are going to look like. I have watched several unhappy lives unfold as a parent defines expectations in precise detail, dedicating all available energy to making sure everybody follows that plan. According to my own observation, fate just thinks that's a hoot.

Better to leave the defining of detail to the last minute, as life has a way of providing critical information late in the game. I think the best anyone can be for themselves, and the best that parents can hope for children, is to be somebody who uses their unique life to contribute to the well-being of others.

It is always possible to live a life of service, regardless of any constraints on the intellect, or on one's physical prowess or even defects in well-laid plans that end up having nothing to do with real life. People inspire each other in myriad ways, and no one is insightful enough to understand how the example they show will affect someone else. Being of service does not happen after years and years of studied preparation…it's a life habit. It is a daily ritual, and it includes everything from the simple manners your parents taught you—be nice, let others go first, say thank you—to the work that you choose to dedicate your life to. Service to others starts with responsibility to yourself and goes back to the Golden Rule: treat other people as you would like for them to treat you.

What makes life meaningful is wanting the best for others. It is a view toward offering your own best…even to people you never met before and may never meet again. Every person comes into this world fully capable of developing their best and giving it right back to the world. Thus, everyone deserves good role models— parents and teachers who recognize the particular gifts in children and help shape those gifts toward service to the world we share.

While the decision to do this is simple, getting it done isn't simple by any means. This takes work. Serious, focused, disciplined work.

And here is one of my favorite examples of shaping a life for service. I think parenting kids toward a life of service is best described as *vision* and *revision*. Strive to accept the details of a child's life as they happen, and help the child develop strength from any and all newly discovered details. I have had the honor of living with a world's master at this in my sister Anne Fletcher Souder.

Anne doesn't impose her worries or what she might think would be perfect. She accepts what is. And because of her attitude and that of my brother-in-law Jay Souder, my nephew Alec Souder is a model of service to the world from a person whose gifts are unconventional.

My family has been blessed with a lot of things over the generations, including the ability to cope well with the fact that many of us inherited and carry a chromosomal disorder known as "Fragile X" which in many cases has passed on to our children. Fragile X is the world's single most prevalent cause of inherited mental impairment and the syndrome's ill effects multiply with each generation. Although I can count 15 of us on my mom's side of the family who carry or are affected by Fragile X, we knew nothing of its existence until about 1995. The same is true for most affected families, as Fragile X has only recently been identified and better understood. Its affects can look quite similar to autism, and it is now considered to be a gateway to understanding the autism spectrum, as the specific protein lack in the brain which causes the disorder has been identified. Identifying the absent protein means we can reasonably hope for the means to a cure or at least amelioration…and that hoped for miracle has become a serious family project.

We discovered that my sister's son Alec was affected by Fragile X when both he and my daughter Annie Graham (named for my sister Anne) were about four years old. We knew that something was amiss because while Alec was a few months older than Annie, he was not reaching developmental milestones at the expected rate.

Because Fragile X was not well understood by the medical community at that time, my sister struggled to find an appropriate diagnosis. At the same time, one of my cousins who is the daughter of my mom's twin was also having concerns about her own two boys. Megan Hamsa Massey was first to discover that the Fragile X diagnosis applied to both of her toddlers, and she has co-authored a book titled *Dear Megan* about that experience. She and her dear friend Mary Beth Busby published and commented on the letters they wrote to each other about raising boys affected by Fragile X. It's a fabulous gift, and if you are somebody or know somebody who is living through this experience of raising children with special needs, I highly recommend it.

As Megan tells people, the best analogy she ever heard was comparing the experience of having and raising her sons to having planned the trip of a lifetime to Italy to see the sights of Rome, Florence, Venice…all the fabulous cities of art, light and romance. The story goes that the tickets are purchased, the airplane is boarded, the flight is great and then, instead of disembarking in Rome, you're in Amsterdam. And while the Netherlands are lovely, you wanted to go to Italy. You had your heart set on Italy and believed that is where your trip of a lifetime would take you. Instead, you learn to navigate and appreciate the wonders of Amsterdam.

My sister had to learn to appreciate Amsterdam.

When Anne had Alec's blood tested for evidence of Fragile X, all of us held our breath. By this time, we were fairly certain that our mothers were carriers, that our grandmother had likely been a carrier and that my great grandmother had been a carrier as well. It explained some patterns in the family that had always been somewhat mysterious, including a great uncle who was affected by an unknown condition that made him unable to live independently. And it was certainly explaining what seemed like a sudden epidemic of slow development in children born to the women in my generation.

It is really difficult for me to explain how I felt during this time. I knew that my children were most likely not affected, because they were developing according to expectation and by that time were 4 and 6 years old. As we came to realize that our family was quite likely passing this condition on from generation to generation, I simply figured that my mother had not passed it on to me, and I was so grateful for the sake of my children that they had not been in danger.

But it wasn't that simple. After Alec's tests came back positive, marking our family as a significant carrier family, it was recommended that all of us be tested to see exactly how many of us were carrying or affected by Fragile X. And being our family, if there was a way to turn this very unwelcome news into a cause we could attack, you can bet that everybody was in on the cause. I had my blood drawn, and we notified my children's father and step-mom, John and Kathleen Graham, that we had received this news and were awaiting my results in order to see if our children would need testing as well. To a person, all of us were certain that testing me was perfunctory.

In the midst of breath-holding and test-result waiting, I must digress. Having disclosed the presence of a former husband and step-mother to my children, I want to encourage you to keep reading by saying that I have been blessed with two amazing other-wives (Kathleen Graham, who is my children's stepmother, and Mary Keegan, who is my stepchildren's mother) and a family that never "broke" after our divorces. We became something of a local phenomenon by minimizing the ill-effects of divorce on ourselves and our children. For now, I will only say I believe far more people have this multiple-family benefit to their lives than is generally acknowledged. And it is a huge benefit.

When we told the Grahams what was going on, they were immediately as engaged in finding a solution and offering support to Anne and Jay for Alec as we all were. One by one, my mom, her sisters and my cousins who had been tested were getting their test results back, and finding that a significant number of us were affected. When I got a call from the genetic center, I was absolutely certain that I would hear I was not a carrier, because I had two children who clearly were not affected and that had not been the case in our other families.

But that's not what I heard.

In fact, I am a carrier, and to a degree that would have deeply affected my children had they inherited this particular X chromosome from me. That news struck me harder than anything I have ever heard or ever expect to hear. How was this even possible?

I already felt terribly guilty about the fact that my sister had this to deal with in her life and I did not. Annie and I had been very close growing up, in spite of the fact that her arrival disrupted my center of attention status since my mother divorced when I was a baby and married the man who became my adored and legal father when I was three.

Life had made me very comfortable with people from day one, and in fact it is fair to say I sought their attention from day one, presuming they would immediately understand that I was worthy of their time. Annie arrived in the world with a far less invasive or presumptive attitude about people's attention. She didn't really want it. Her shy demeanor made me very protective of her, especially after she joined me in grade school… albeit four years behind. So for our entire lives I had felt it was my job to secure her place in the world. This was not something she sought, by the way, and I am quite sure I was a royal pain for her on any number of occasions. And now, come to find out that not only were my children not affected by Fragile X, but by rights—or odds—at least one of them should have been.

I really lost faith in a world I thought I understood right up until then. The news precipitated a period of serious questioning for me, as I could not fathom the meaning or depth of this unfairness. I was busy at this point getting both Annie and Justin tested, which meant having to tell their father and stepmother that there was a good possibility they were carriers. Again, this was something both John and Kathleen handled with grace. And as it turned out, neither one of my children is a carrier or affected.

Finding out they were not affected was obviously a huge relief. And I was angry for being relieved, angry about all of it. It's my guess that many people arrive at junctures similar to this one in their lives where they want to ask The Great Unseen Plan Maker one question: "What in the hell are you thinking?"

I take great joy in my children and always have. It is not solely a mother's pride to say they are pretty amazing people, which is something that I did not create but will take credit for an assist. I spent quite a few weeks not talking about this, being angry that what seemed to be blind chance had liberated my children's lives and constrained my nephews'. I just didn't get it. I frankly don't get it still, and I don't plan on getting it.

Instead, I found peace with it in an unlikely moment. When I finally was capable of telling friends this news, I was sharing the fact that my children were not affected, and somebody innocently said, "Oh, thank God." It was meant to be graceful, I understand.

But I was furious.

My response was, "I don't think God afflicted Alec any more than I believe that He spared Annie and Justin. I think they all have the gifts they need for now. I think He gave them the grace to use whatever measure of ability they have. I think that is everybody's gift."

And that is what I believe…that there is little difference in the "value" of service one is capable of giving in the world. The value comes in the attitude to be of service in the first place, and in serving according to the gifts that were granted. In my children's cases, they have gifts of the intellect that are unique to them, but more common, and that will allow for more conventional leadership. What Alec has is very unconventional intellect, but a huge heart and a massive ability to support the community he is part of.

I am a strenuous believer in the obligation of parents (or those who play any active role in a child's life) to push those children toward service for others. It is the only thing that makes sense to me. And in order for children to play out that role according to their abilities, they must be taught to develop whatever gifts they have. I, for one, cannot settle for mediocre, and cannot fear to allow their struggle.

My sister and I did not differ in our belief that our children would serve the world in ways equally valuable. The biggest difference has been in the time and energy that being their parents requires. It is ridiculous to say that I spent anywhere near the time, frustration, energy, research, or just blood, sweat and tears that is required to give a person like Alec every possible opportunity to develop the gifts that he has. And my sister and her husband Jay have been heroic. Not only because they fought for what Alec would need, but because they used Alec's experience as a way to raise awareness and resources for many, many other children like Alec. They turned their support for Alec into support for an entire community.

And Alec is turning into somebody with a great gift for supporting his own community. Alec just turned 21, (or as he explained, "Yeah, that's a big number, Aunt Lisa.") and has been working at Fry's Marketplace as well as serving as his Horizon High School football team's "hydration manager" for the past four years. We figure they can't do without him now, even after graduation, because the world has no better team mascot.

Alec's struggle with Fragile X means he deals with people through a sometimes thick film of social anxiety, but he overcomes all of that for his team. Football season means long work days and nights, but Alec is deeply invested in his service. And he has this gift of service due to exceptional navigation on his parents' part.

One of the other great gifts my brother-in-law has is being an exceptional speaker, and he often encourages parents to expect more than they think is possible by sharing his own moment of insight about the hubris and constraints held by those of us with a typical intellect. Here is that story.

Jay and Annie always made sure that Alec had wonderful teachers. As with every child's education, the teacher is everything. Everything. So Alec had this wonderful pre-school arts instructor at a school for those with special needs, who expected great things of all her students, and exposed them to the great artists and ideas that have inspired our hearts through the ages.

Jay was working with Alec at home one day when he was only about four, paying close attention to Alec's small motor skills by constructing block buildings, LEGOs, etc. After getting Alec started, Jay left the room to read the paper in his study. After a few moments Alec walked in with a Mr. Potato Head toy, fully stuffed with pieces in every hole. It seemed that Alec's fine motor skills were great…but Mr. Potato Head had an ear where a nose should've been and the eyes were at lip level. Jay was devastated.

All Jay could think was that Alec was making great progress using his hands but there was so much work to do on the intellect. "Honey, Mr. Potato Head's ears go on the sides of his head, and see his lips? They go here where you have his eyes."

And Alec—who used very few words at this age—just stared at his father, exasperated. Then he said, "No, Daddy! It's a Picasso Potato Head!"

As Jay described his reaction: "Oh. Wow."

How ready we are to underestimate the capacity of any child, based on what is "known" about their abilities.

And this is true risk for all of us, and all of our children.

Our family's experience with Fragile X made me fairly radical about my belief that every child arrives capable of giving their best in service to others, and that doing so is what provides value to their lives. It has been amazing to me to observe the intensity with which special needs children and adults seek to serve others. Even more so, I have learned what it is to be a great parent by watching Anne and Jay set a very high bar for my nephew Alec, even when doing so has had to drain them of nearly every available emotional resource.

It's a perspective I draw on every day, and it inspires me far more than they know.

It has also added to my impatient nature...something I may not have needed encouragement for. I have zero tolerance for those who choose a life of indifference when they come equipped with everything they need to be productive, intellectually robust and a great contributor to the community and world. And I think that almost all of us arrive here with what we need. This isn't about all of us reaching the same "bar"; it's about stretching our own boundaries. So the most frustrated I ever get is watching as parents, teachers or caregivers decide to define children by perceived limitations before testing the limits of what is possible. Or they decide not to risk a child's frustration, which *always* accompanies stretching one's boundaries, because they have so identified with the child's angst that they perceive the child's struggle as their own pain and they can't endure it.

Any child's life is going to be a struggle to one degree or another. It needs to be, and parents, teachers and other caregivers should strive to accept that many of the biggest influencers on children will be out of our control. Instead, the focus must be on what can be controlled and on the best available choices. Anyone can choose their outlook, expectations, and willingness to seize a moment and wring every bit of joy and purpose possible from any and all conditions.

Raising the next generation of children is both an absolute joy and a nearly unbearable burden. It is our shared job as adults, regardless of whether the kids come through us or not. Look around, they're all over the place, these kids! I had the great gift of growing up in a family where everybody I knew understood that and was committed to it. They had choices for how the world would affect the children in their care, and they taught me to value the choices that I had as well.

I did not have and did not need a picture perfect, smooth and glossy, disruption-free existence. What I had—and have—is a real life. And I know that when life is at its most threatening, I am able to exercise choices…mostly because I was taught to choose environments where I could best serve my purpose, and in part because I flat out had access to the choices I knew would make a difference for me or for my family.

And that has created a very full, very blessed life indeed. The belief that I have a right to choose a unique and happy path for myself and for my family is a significant gift. But that belief is nothing without the ability to act on it. And I have had that access; sometimes just because I believed that I did.

So now, ensuring that others have the same access to the choices that I have had is what gets me up in the morning. Mostly I do that where education is concerned, but I figure why waste a good obsession…I have learned to apply the principle everywhere.

I am pretty sure that is the reason I am around to get up in the morning in the first place.

Chapter Four

The Choice of Fathers

One of the other reasons I am here to get up in the morning is Daphne Young Fletcher. Daphne is my mother, and she is the greatest example of both choosing and creating environments that will be good for kids that I have ever met. Actually, my mother is a great example of lots of things, and there is a reason that my children have an expression "WWDD?" (what would Daphne do?) knocking-off the "WWJD" (what would Jesus do?) bracelets that folks wore a few years back.

Hopefully, Jesus has the sense of humor I suspect He does. Actually, I am relying on His hearty sense of humor about a lot of things, so…fingers crossed.

At any rate, the kids coined this term as they got older and began to see past simple adoration and to recognize the graceful genius that is my mother. It looks easy to be my mom, because she wants you to think that. It hasn't always been, and I came face to face with one of her most challenging choices about 10 years ago when I finally met my biological father.

Before you read this story, I need for you to understand something that became even more clear to me after I wrote this book and submitted it to Pat…my wonderful lifetime friend and editor. She told me that I had not qualified who I was referring to when I spoke of my "father." We then both realized that I only ever use the term for my real father, the man who adopted and raised me.

And that merely reflects truth. Your parents are the people who not only bring you into the family, but then do the day-to-day work of introducing you to the world. Your mother, your father, your step-parents... all of those people earn a right to be called your parent over a very long time and through all sorts of joys and sorrows. Being somebody's parent is an honor and a solemn responsibility. I only have one father; but I did briefly meet the man who gave up the original job.

He wasn't a part of my life, and I even hesitated to tell this story because it feels like doing so adds unmerited consequence and weight to something I consider more of a... feather.

While I never knew much about the person...I did know a lot about the story. My mother *created* it for the benefit of me and for my brother. What I came to understand was that my mother's actions and words transformed what could have been an ungainly ostrich in our lives...into more of a lovely, light and fairly inconsequential feather.

To start with the moral of the story before the story itself: Amazing parents shape their own lives around the needs of their children. They don't dwell on their own disappointments; they look constantly to what will work best for their children. It's what my parents did, and it's a beautiful thing.

So... here's my feather of a story:

The call was irresistible. It was 2002 and I was in Colorado Springs attending a meeting of Secretary of Education Rod Paige's Commission on Title IX, where we were attempting to lessen the tensions of fully supporting women in college level sports. Secretary Paige had appointed me to the commission via a very brief conversation with Margaret Spellings, who later became Secretary of Education herself but at that time was Domestic Policy Advisor to President George W. Bush.

The case was made simply, "Lisa, we need to throw somebody we trust into this." Secretary Spellings is a no bullshit, get-to-the-point woman. I'm a fan. Our conversation continued.

"Margaret, I don't really understand the Title IX food fight. I think everybody's right."

"Perfect. Us too. It's a commission for God's sake. Do what seems like the right thing."

And that was the full scope of our in-depth discussion. I loved reading all the comments about the commission later from supposed insiders who "knew" I had been sent by the Bush administration to promote an anti-woman agenda.

I am a woman, of course, and our daughter Annie played elite soccer. I am a huge fan of Title IX and its requirements, and supported it on the panel. I just had a problem with some of the penalties that were assessed on universities when after a great deal of effort and expense they simply had more men than women commit to play a sport. Agreeing with both sides on an issue like this makes you the friend of neither.

At any rate, I was sitting in a hotel room after the meeting when I got a call from my husband. I figured he'd want to know who I pissed off that day.

"Hey there!"

"Hey…I have some news for you." His voice was not playful. This is a horrifying moment when you are on the road and away from your kids.

"Is everything okay?"

"Yes, yes. I just talked to Rich." Rich is my brother.

"And?"

"He is in touch with Harris."

Silence on my end. There's only one Harris. He's my biological father.

"Lisa?"

"I'm here." I'm crying. Why am I crying? "I wish you were here."

"I know. Me too." More silence. "He wants you to call him."

"Rich?"

"Harris."

"Oh. God." As in please help me. "Am I happy about this?"

"I don't know...yes. You wanted to know if he was alive or dead. He's alive. Up to you what you do now."

He's alive? He's alive. He had not tried to reach me or my brother for decades, and now he's alive. Death I could have understood more easily. It's harder to get in touch.

I am not a big tears person, but I am now crying again and I am annoyed to be crying again. I am not sure Harris deserves my exertion.

"We both know I am going to call him." This admission makes me more miserable.

I aspire to live the credo of my chosen father and my husband: DO. NOT. FORGET. They believe in the covenant of appropriate behavior. They respect the line. They believe that the people who hurt you cross that line on purpose. They remember who does it. They don't ever allow them close enough to cross that line again. As in: fool me once, shame on you; fool me twice, shame on me. Actually, fooling either one of these favorite guys of mine twice is nearly impossible.

I drive them both crazy. I don't respect the power of the line. I insist that everybody gets along. I don't just ignore the line, I stand there for most of my life, inviting people who dislike each other intensely to cross over and hug it out. I honestly forget when people are cruel to me...it passes, we live through it, and I am most likely to throw a party celebrating the moment. It happens a lot. It is fair to call it a hallmark of my character. It is exhausting to people who love me. Fool me once, shame on you; fool me twice—let's talk about it! What are you doing to me? Why am I allowing this? Shall we have coffee and discuss?

"Yes. We both know you will call." Silence yet again. But I hear him smile. "You know you can wait to call until you get home. I'll stand by with the Bushmills and a shot glass."

We are an Irish family by blood and by practice. I am now smiling into tears and a cell phone. I have the world's greatest husband.

"Lisa?"

"Yep."

"Call your brother."

So that was indeed an irresistible call, and I did call my brother, and we did eventually head out to meet Harris in San Francisco. But not to find a father. We already had a father who had chosen us.

Actually, we chose each other. My mother says the proposal actually came from me while we were all in Palm Springs with my grandparents. As my mother's then-beau was throwing 2-year-old me up and down in the pool, I apparently decided we had a winner.

"Can you be our new Daddy?"

Other than mortifying my mother, it was one of life's great calls. I like to think I have an eye for perfection.

Looking back at it now, I marvel at my dad's willingness to join the intensity that is our family. I can only understand his willingness by knowing my mother, who is one of the most beautiful women you'll ever meet. In every way. But even so, my respect for my father has increased over the years as I understand what he had to deal with in order to make us his family.

Including Harris.

Rich and I were the happy products of what must have been a genuinely unhappy situation for my mother. What either one of us knew about Harris as we grew up, we knew from my mother. She said only that she and Harris married young. After I was born, she said, Harris decided he could not handle the responsibilities of family, and he severed all ties.

But she constantly emphasized that he had loved us tremendously. We were the only thing that made him happy. He was just so proud of us. It is funny to me now that this explanation sufficed when I was a child, but it did. I thought it was odd and vaguely sad, but I never felt I had lost anything. I had a real father who loved me and saw me every day.

In fact the only occasion I can remember feeling I wanted to see Harris, or told my mother so, I was four years old and had been put in time-out yet again. I spent a lot of time there, and was looking for a rescue. I thought maybe good old what's-his-name would care that his daughter was being imprisoned.

"I want my other-father!" I shouted from behind the mesh crib curtain.

My mother whipped around, duly horrified. "What are you talking about? You have never even met him."

"But *he* loves me."

Actually, this story about Harris's love for us sprang from a very generous nature on my mom's part. After meeting Harris as an adult, I know the truth of the matter was a bit more complicated than my mother's explanation, which was absolutely consistent with her ongoing campaign to make sure we saw ourselves as lovable. Her brief marriage to Harris had been no picnic, and it came to an abrupt end in late 1959, shortly after I arrived on the scene the summer before.

My parents had been living in Palo Alto because Harris was enrolled at Stanford University, pursuing an MBA after completing his law degree at the University of Nebraska and failing to focus on the seemingly obvious next steps of passing the state bar exams and becoming employed. The family consensus…well, my mother's family consensus—you should be getting the picture here that we are a maternal monopoly—was that having failed to become an attorney, Harris should attain the business acumen essential to help run the family newspaper.

My mother's side of our family has these deep roots I have described for you in Nebraska...including a former territorial governor, a state Supreme Court justice and two U.S. senators. As I mentioned earlier, my great-great grandfather Gilbert Hitchcock had not only been a U.S. senator during the Wilson years, he was also the owner and publisher of the *Omaha World-Herald*. Trust me, I often reflect on how nice it would have been to own the state's largest newspaper when I was in public office. I am led to believe there was no breach of editorial protocol, and a review of Gilbert's electoral win/loss record would seem to validate that view. All the same, though...

The *Omaha World-Herald* remained a family newspaper business from the time Gilbert founded it in 1885, up until we sold the newspaper to Omaha business leader Peter Kiewit in 1963. As a sidelight, that newspaper is still world-class and one of very few newspapers actually owned by its employees until very recently. In December of 2011, it was purchased by Warren Buffet, something my grandmother would heartily approve of as he is "local," which she felt all newspapers had to be. In the early 1960s, my grandmother had to fight tooth and nail to keep the paper from being amalgamated out of its local mission by the media mogul William Randolph Hearst. Or as she lovingly described him to me, "That bastard."

During the 1950s, we still owned the newspaper and the family was experiencing a bit of a kerfuffle over who would take the helm at the paper after my great-grandfather Henry Doorly. As often happens, there were factions jockeying for position, and since Harris seemed highly personable and bright (if a tad unfocused), my grandparents joined with Harris's parents to support his acquisition of the skills it would take to manage the paper.

So with a great deal of parental support and investment, out to California and into Stanford went my parents, with Harris in pursuit of an MBA, or so my mother and the rest of the family believed.

In fact, as he would recount for my brother, my husband and I in unedited detail during our one visit to see him, Harris found Stanford University to be intellectually stifling and no competition for the philosophically beguiling world of the beatniks up the road in San Francisco. Harris's take on this was that he was deeply engaged in living out the philosophies of Ayn Rand and world actualization through realized self-interest.

My personal take on this now is that he excelled solely in the pursuit of self-interest. His obsession with personal realization extended to no others, and I had no contact with him for the entirety of my 40 some-odd years to that point.

Until the call.

After my brother and I decided that we would go visit Harris in San Francisco, accompanied by my husband as a human shield, Harris sent us a *rendez-vous* address. As I was sitting in my home office with our son Justin one day, I looked it up on the Internet, and was stunned to find that the Dalt Hotel Harris directed us to was not a hotel at all; I believe they referred to themselves as low-income housing. The story I was getting from the web site made clear that the Dalt could be better understood as a homeless shelter.

My son was nearby watching me click through screen after screen of the Dalt Hotel site and asked, "Mom, what are you looking for?" Justin was 13, but his adolescent disinterest in parents had parked itself elsewhere for the moment. He wanted to know what I thought I could find by endless gazing at pictures of the Dalt.

"I don't know. I guess I want to understand what kind of choices would make this place his home address. He had every opportunity. He had everything. I mean...this is not a hard luck story, this is an active choice."

"Well, whatever he is, that picture isn't going to tell you. Interesting that's where he wants you to meet him, though."

Indeed. So out to San Francisco and to the Dalt we went, me, John and my brother, navigating the Tenderloin district of San Francisco until we reached the correct address.

It was a bit difficult to tell if we were in exactly the right spot as we stepped inside, as the most prominent sign at the reception booth inside the lobby read: "BULLETPROOF GLASS." Apparently, we needed to know that more than the name of the woman who was encased in it and was involved in reviewing our identification. No name plate was posted, and no eye contact was made with us by the receptionist. This unnerved me. When I am out of my element, I rely on other people's eyes to confirm my existence. She kept all of us guessing.

Once we were logged in, all I could make my brain focus on was the fact that she needed a picture ID from each of us but she never once looked at our faces. What's the point? She read "Harris Poley" in the line where we had written our destination, and pointed to the stairs. "Room's that way."

My bother Rich looked at me, then put his arm around me and we turned toward the stairs. My husband put his hands on both of our backs and steered us through the overly bright lobby. The facility looked about the way I guessed it would from the website. Stark. After studying that site for a month, I had hoped it would be so familiar that actually walking in would not feel so surreal. No such luck.

As we proceeded, I reflected that the man I was walking upstairs to meet probably helped to create my passion for maximizing the gifts I was given just by serving as an example of how to throw them away. I didn't know Harris Poley well enough to know what life contributions he made, so in order to be overly generous, let me admit that my assumptions about his choices might have been off base. Possible, but not likely. I concluded that when a person begins life with abundant personal gifts and a supportive family, but ends up living off the charity of a community that he should have been contributing to, then that person has chosen to be less than they were meant to be.

So I was a bit conflicted walking up those stairs. Without my husband's steadily urging hand on my back, I may have succumbed to the increasingly obnoxious voice in my head: "Oh, yoo-hoo, Mrs. I-Can-Handle-This! Perhaps it has escaped your memory, but the gentleman you are going to see has not known or cared where you were for the past 43 years, so why do you care where and how and who he is? Is this smart? Ever heard of self-respect? Why are you here?"

I didn't know. The best I could come up with was that he was still alive and he'd asked us to visit. Add the fact that unfinished family business inspires me. It's such a rich opportunity for dialogue and new understanding! Or so I always hope.

As we stood outside his room at the Dalt waiting for the door to open, I had not yet heard his version of life events and had no idea what I would do or how I would feel after this long-delayed introduction. The whole evening is a memory that still hangs in isolated suspension, unattached to much else; the hours that followed did very little to help me put this relationship into the context of my life.

The man we were meeting at the door had been absent to my brother and me. He spent a lifetime being absent from his *entire* family. He had lived the antithesis of my very close family life, even though I knew from having been in distant touch with his brothers that his immediate family was, like mine, a very close group. Harris chose a life apart from family interaction and dedicated himself to the singular pursuit of his own interests.

Beyond sheer curiosity to meet the man, I wondered if he had truly lived a life guided by this objectivist ideology. My political leanings run strongly enough to libertarian that I wondered if perhaps living out that philosophy could result in a compelling story—and I was open to hearing it. I will admit deep skepticism from the start, however, based on my inability to reconcile Ayn Rand's ideas being channeled through a person dependent on the public for his housing. It felt stunningly unromantic.

When the door finally opened, the gentleman who stood there was familiar only because he looked like an older and more angular version of my brother, an inescapable first impression. He had long grey hair which looked freshly washed, and he had pulled it back into a pony tail. His clothes were worn but not threadbare, save for the fact that his suspenders weren't decorative and were serving in lieu of the waistband button of his trousers, which was missing.

His room at the Dalt was just that. A room. He lived in a small room with a cardboard packing box that served as a bedside table, holding condiments for the meals he must have preferred to eat in his room. There was a Formica slab attached to the wall which served as a desk for his computer, which he informed us he was using to start his latest business venture.

Sure, okay.

The opposite wall held his narrow bed and a tall bookshelf, overflowing with books. I would have liked to have spent more time reviewing titles in order to get a sense of the man, but after a cursory review I spotted more than a few books about sex. As it happens, he was ultimately not going to be gracious enough to respect my Episcopalian preference to avoid discussions of other people's sexual intimacy. But at this early stage in the evening I was still able to avert my eyes away from the books and the topic, and did. So I can't say what other topics he was pursuing. I have no doubt he was a highly literate guy.

I suppose it was to his credit that he seemed unapologetic about the humble nature of his combination reception area-bedroom-kitchen-library-8 x 12-foot living space. I sat next to him on his bed, my brother took the available chair, and my husband remained standing. John assumed the military stance that he automatically adopts after appointing himself sentry of a situation. I don't know if he does this on purpose or if he even knows that he does it, but it's intimidating. John spent much of his life serving our country in various roles for the military, usually doing work with the word "intelligence" attached somewhere. He's taken on lots of jobs I know better than to ask about. I tell people not to spill their guts to John at a bar late in the evening thinking the combination of informality and liquor will mean all's forgotten in the morning. The man's a trained, um, listener, and those drinks you think he's having will never get him drunk. He will remember. Everything.

He's handy.

And he was an essential addition to this increasingly surreal moment, a moment that still hangs unencumbered in my head. Harris was looking closely at Rich and me, telling us he can still see the children we were when he last saw us. And he was highlighting whatever favorable features we had with their similarity to his own. He talked a bit about having lived with us in the small house on Oxford Street in Palo Alto, and how my mother was so freaked out when he let Richie roam further than across the street to see his friend. For your information, "across the street" means Oxford, and from there, the next stop is El Camino Real, then and now the major thoroughfare in the city. Seeing her two year old toddle that direction was indeed a good time to freak out. Score one for mom.

What was remarkable about the evening was our nearly immediate realization that Harris was not going to ask us…about us. He wanted to tell *his* story, and began his narrative as we sat in his room for a bit, prior to the plans we'd made with him for dinner. Just as we were getting ready to head out, he was alluding to various jobs he had taken on over the years, including one as director of a tax policy network. He was discussing his commitment to the principles we knew he felt strongly about, and then he took my breath away by telling us that there was only one organization he still gave money to because he believed in the honesty of their mission.

Now, never mind the dissonance involved in writing checks for charitable contributions from a table in the homeless shelter. He said that the only honest organization he knew of that had maintained principle was the Milton and Rose Friedman Foundation. He saw me look at John, and

John said, "Lisa and I know the Friedmans. Milton has been a wonderful mentor to Lisa."

In fact, one of the great honors of my life was being presented a few years before this meeting with the Friedman Foundation's first leadership award for my work to advance school choice. Milton and Rose had come out to Phoenix from San Francisco to personally present that to me, and John and I had subsequently spent time with the Friedmans in their beautiful home on Nob Hill. This coincidence was remarkable to me, and when John shared the story with Harris, he was visibly pleased, as he replied: "Well, see? You get these things started and you don't ever know how much good you are doing!"

I am not sure if the "things" Harris was referring to were me or the foundation, but please note the glory belonged to him.

After this short visit, we headed out for dinner. We told Harris to pick somewhere he liked, thinking that he would choose a location close to his residence. Wrong. Harris wanted to go to a restaurant that his friend and iconic city personality Ed Moose had started years ago. Moose's was a truly great place in San Francisco. And Mr. Moose devoted much of his own time and resource to the underserved in San Francisco. Unfortunately, the city lost the man and the restaurant just a few years ago.

I'd like to say we learned some useful things about Harris and about our mother and ourselves over dinner. I'd like to, but that implies understanding. We heard a lot, but I learned very little. And partially because the stories Harris chose to share were not stories a father would typically share with his kids...even if he had actually known his kids for some time.

As the evening wore on, I realized that the pictures I had brought of my children, his grandchildren, were going to stay in my purse. At first I was hurt that he didn't ask about them, but then instinct led me to shelter my kids from this moment. What I didn't realize then was that I would later decide to shelter them from Harris entirely. During the dinner itself,

Simple Choices

I was not focused on any future plans; I was just trying to get through the evening.

Harris regaled us with bawdy highlights in his life. He began by describing the last night he saw us as a family, which ended with his packed car driving away from the house he shared with my mother in Palo Alto to a life he would begin and end in San Francisco. The details he shared of his life were inconsistent and sketchy, punctuated by a need to share information I would rather not have known. Okay, here's an example.

Apparently, he began a relationship with a "professional" woman who worked out of the local bar, based in part on his need for housing (obviously a repetitive life theme). This relationship ended when she started buying clothes for him, indicating an emotional attachment and thus violating his now fully developed life credo. Those of you who've read Atlas Shrugged by Ayn Rand will recognize his chanting of John Galt's oath, "I swear—by my Life and my love of it—that I will never live for the sake of another man, nor ask another man to live for mine."

WHAT???!!! is what I thought to myself, as public scenes are not my thing. Internally, however, my speech was fabulous:

"Okay, darlin', perhaps it has escaped you, but your foyer with the lovely bullet-proofed receptionist…is supported by the public. The room you live in…is being subsidized and maintained by folks whose compassion extends to you. And back in the day…accepting this woman's housing and—ahem—other gifts that met your needs, is a dependency you claim to abhor. Furthermore, accepting your family's financial support while you jumped from grad school to grad school with a wife and children, committing to none of them…was equally as dependent. You were born on third base, thought you hit a triple, and have basically been asking people to live for your sake all your life, as far as I can tell."

But I didn't say any of that. Instead, I sought a bit of shelter in an objective observer's stance, drew on my glass of wine and thought of Henry David Thoreau's book, *Walden; or, Life in the Woods*. Harris's

The Choice of Fathers

story was not uninteresting, and it detailed the life of somebody who believed they were forging a truly unique and important path. I could take him no more seriously than I take Thoreau's perspective on the virtues of an isolated, solitary life. Thoreau's isolation amounted to two of the eight years he took to write the book, and the entire period was punctuated by support from his friends and runs home so his mother could do his laundry. I was listening to an extreme version of the same syndrome.

I suppose the new clothes this woman had been trying to force on Harris represented a visible sign of dependence; gifts of clothing happened to be where he drew the line. Perhaps the lack of a button on his pants that evening was simply a declaration of independence. His life story centered on his success in living a pure ideology: Nobody had been able to tie him down or make him less than he was meant to be. Looking the part of a complete independent seemed to be important to him. Perhaps that was the answer to my son Justin's query about why he wanted us to meet him in his home at the Dalt; he was thriving in an environment that could break a lesser man.

There was a repetitive figure in his litany of those who had lacked appreciation for the art form that was his life. This would be my grandmother... the one nicknamed "Nails." By this point in the dinner, I was enormously cheered by the thought of any conversation that would have occurred between my grandmother and this man. In fact, Harris had paused his hour-long monologue to await our agreement that my grandmother's intervention to keep him out of our lives had been a detestable act. As I think both my brother and I had at that moment never loved our bad-ass grandmother more, the conversation went silent.

Then, John erupted. "Seriously, Harris, what the *fuck* happened?" It's interrogation-John to the rescue. My husband John is a really big guy. With a really big voice. Our children call him The Big Giant Head, and that voice of his has been a serious results-producer over the years.

John grilled Harris on what would cause a man raised with the advantages he had to go "off the grid," abandon his children and not seek

Simple Choices

them out over a period of 40 some-odd years. As John pointed out, his seeming nemesis, my grandmother, had long since passed over, and all of us were in the phone book. Harris didn't flinch, which is impressive, and he provided a litany of excuses. But by then we had allowed Harris so much time to define himself for us I had developed the unvarnished picture.

I knew what I needed to know. There wasn't going to be a compelling life story. We would not be able to walk away thinking that even though he had not kept in touch with us, he had accomplished such amazing work that one could at least appreciate his contributions. Neither would we hear any desire on his part to know our lives, what interested us, what we had done, cared about or learned along the way.

After finishing the longest dinner of my life, we dropped Harris back at Dalt with promises to stay in touch and headed back to our hotel. (True to our promise, Rich and I did stay in touch with Harris via email just long enough to hear that he needed money from each of us as a stake in his newest venture. The moment reminded me of my husband's favorite coffee mug, which says *"CONSISTENCY: it's only a virtue if you aren't a screw-up".*)

As we arrived back at our hotel that night, my brother and I shuffled out of the cab and went straight for the elevator to our rooms. John was incredulous. "Wait," he said. "Are you kidding me?? You think you're just going to bed? Oh no. There is no way. You two drag me out here to play bouncer for your totally dysfunctional deadbeat-dad dinner, and then you just want to call it a day? Huh-uh. There is a bar right here, and we are going in. And we are going to sit at that bar. And we are going to have a drink. Personally, I am having two drinks. And then we are going to *talk*. Because your family is always just a little crazy and I put up with you guys, but that...*that* was bizarre."

So we did go in to the bar, and we did have a drink. Or two. And finally, we got past the shock, or surprise, or whatever it is when you find out for sure that the romantic fantasy you flirted with about an honorable loner pining away for you all these years was just that— fantasy. Once past that, we could truly appreciate how inappropriate most of the evening had been. Deeply, completely, unexpectedly inappropriate.

We laughed until the bar closed. I love my family's coping skills.

So I can cope, but I still maintain my obsessions. And one of my favorite (occasionally unhealthy) obsessions is my belief that all family members can, should and ultimately will enjoy the hell out of being together. My children can spell out the details of this obsession for you better than I can. But let me just tell you that once I discovered that Harris was alive…Yahtzee! A new project! I went to work creating fantasy scenarios for how we could include him in events with the children, gradually bringing him back into a family fold.

This illusion was shattered for me as John and I were driving from the airport to pick up our children after returning from the San Francisco encounter. Justin and Annie were about 10 and 13 at the time, and were at their Graham house. We had gotten all the way back to Phoenix and nearly to the Grahams' before the weight of the encounter with Harris struck me and I began to cry.

"Oh, Lisa." John looked over to see the tears. "Can I just say I have been waiting about 36 hours for this?"

The day after meeting Harris, I had a business meeting and there just hadn't been time to process the experience.

I met John's eyes and said, "I just realized I am not sure how to introduce such an asshole to our children."

At this, John literally pulled the car off the road and turned it off. He turned to face me directly. "Look at me. That is never, ever going to happen. There is nothing good that can come from those kids meeting a man they don't know, they don't miss and who doesn't deserve them. I know what you are thinking. You are family-obsessed. This man is not family and I am so sorry. I think we just say as little as we can get away with to the children and then you and I can deal with you. You can stay in touch with him if you want. I don't think it's a good idea, but that's up to you. The children are something else entirely and I think John and Kathleen would feel the same way."

My husband is a really clear guy, and I needed to hear this and to experience what it felt like to absolutely shut down any opportunity for a family member to play the role of prodigal son.

It didn't feel good. It did feel right.

When we reached the Graham's house, the children were happy to see us, and they were quite uninterested in hearing about Harris. They were not lacking for wonderful grandfathers. We did escape the kids long enough to visit privately with the Grahams and all agreed that there would be no contact between the children and Harris. He had lost his rights decades ago, and then he lost them all over again during dinner.

Friends have since asked me if I thought he was disordered or alcoholic, wanting to understand Harris by believing he suffered from a delusional state. I honestly do not believe that was the case. I think that it is possible to choose to serve only yourself, and I think doing so for most of a lifetime warps your ability to relate to others and rots your soul. God only knows what it took for Harris to remain a single, resolutely unattached ego. A friend of my mother's recently told me that before he died, Harris had relayed his regret over losing touch with us. I am sorry if he was in pain. But it was clear he had made that choice.

And I would conclude it was the wrong choice but making that judgment haunts me. Despite my personal hurt, I cannot know what Harris brought to the world. I can be grateful that he brought my brother and me into the world, and I know without question that my experience with him – or more precisely without him – shaped my life. So I live at peace with Harris and I wish his soul well.

And I can credit him with contributing to my philosophy: Whoever we are, wherever we are, we live in society with others. I see no shame in seeking support from others, nor any glory in refusing to give it. On a very personal level, my faith doesn't present support for others as optional. The Golden Rule outlined in my New Testament has a correlate edict in nearly every faith: "Do unto others as you would have them do unto you." Easy to say, difficult to do, essential to try.

I see very little charm in the ease of pursuing one's needs above all others, and it's a poisonous choice for those of us who are blessed to raise or care for children. Life as a parent or caregiver is not about you, it's about the child and the choices you must make to keep them safe and capable. I thank God that both of my real parents understood that.

End of story.

Chapter Five
Mother's Choice

I had worked through Harris and his place in my life long before our unexpected trip to see him in San Francisco. I knew that his connection to me would never make complete sense, and it didn't have to. Getting to that point took some therapeutic effort.

Which I really hate admitting because it makes me so normal.

As I shared with you earlier, I have a need to see myself as somebody who manages the traumas of life much better than everybody else. It has never been true…or false, for that matter…I cope as well as I can. But believing I can soar where others might stumble is part of my shtick.

Everyone has shtick, and I find it's best to come clean about what is really driving me. So having done serious, mundane, very human work on putting Harris into perspective, actually meeting him was much less traumatic. *Less.*

What fascinated me after meeting Harris was understanding how my mother created and stuck to her graceful story about Harris loving all of us but not being able to manage us. The truth had been so much more difficult, so much more complicated. And I never knew it. My mom chose to spare us the messy detail, choosing rather to instill in us the belief that Rich and I were Harris's redeeming features.

The only detail about Harris that I got from my mother came from a conversation we had when I was in high school and breaking up with a serious boyfriend. I wanted to know how she knew her marriage to Harris was over. I recall that she turned the story into a life lesson about moving ahead. That is a typical Daphne technique, and it helped me enormously at the time. Moving ahead is exactly what my mother did.

Basically, once my mom discovered that Harris had ceased to attend classes and was enrolled at Stanford in name and cost only, she confronted him. Only mildly upset, he explained to Daphne that his group of San Francisco friends was doing something much more important than attending business school. They were redefining tradition. They were seeking a higher purpose. He wanted her to know that in 1959, what he was doing was What People Do Now. It didn't mean he didn't love my mother. And since he would not be finishing a degree at Stanford, maybe they should divert their resources to buy a coffee house in Santa Cruz where they could host budding intellectuals.

Um...small problem, Harris. Daphne was already engaged in hosting budding intellectuals. One was two, and one was due. Call it bad timing.

Mom was no vapid debutante without a soul, sense of adventure or heart for the intellectual life. She was and is one of the best educated and most interesting women I know. Plus, I know from my grandmother that she and her twin sister Diane were a hell of a lot of fun. Bami frequently recounted the stories of how Daphne and Diane were sent away to National Cathedral boarding school in Washington, D.C. for spending too much time with the local Omaha high school ice hockey team. That stint was followed by a reassignment to Anokia boarding school in California after National Cathedral discovered that the "chauffeur" who picked the girls up for a weekend away at their aunt's home was actually just a boyfriend with a really convincing hat and car.

In spite of being all sorts of good distracting fun, Daphne was also a leader. She was a student government member, class president, lead camper sort of gal... a very solid citizen. She had a path. I do remember her telling me that shortly before her marriage she joined a European tour where she found herself questioning whether the path she was on was the one she truly desired. But that was just a momentary hitch... the match with Harris was a connection of two fine families, two hyper bright young people, all destined for great things. So she decided this new family would be exactly right.

And in the space of an afternoon about five years later, she found herself having to undecide.

In spite of being an educated intellectual and somebody well versed in the current culture, my mother understood something that Harris could not: Individuals are not here just to discover themselves. She believed people were to learn lessons and to become the best they could be so that they could serve others well. She thought societies that persevere do so because generations before them sought to make the world a better place for all who would come later. And, people who are blessed enough to bring children into the world and into their families, have a particular obligation to apply their lives to the next generation. It isn't an option. Or it shouldn't be.

In sharing this story of her divorce with me, my mother came as close as she ever had to faulting Harris and his choices. Maybe she sensed I was old enough to know, maybe she grasped the teachable moment that excellent mothers are famous for seizing. But I clearly recall that she drew a distinction for me between the emerging ethos of the 60's that she felt had claimed Harris, and her own profound sense of obligation to serve others. I don't believe that the 60's spawned narcissism, and I know my mother did not believe that either. But the times did elevate the individual and the pursuit of one's own desires in ways that would comfort somebody already prone to avoiding responsibility. And that lesson of two very different paths to choose from stayed with me. Without even knowing Harris, I chose to follow my mother.

It is part of the maturing process that we move beyond our own immediate desires. We teach our children the significance of patience, we help them understand that what they want might conflict with what is possible or what would be best at the current time. We teach them to balance what they want with what others want, we help them understand

Simple Choices

that looking beyond their own needs to the needs of others is expected. And as we mature, we come to realize that service to others is actually its own reinforcement. With growing empathy comes a deepening understanding of the magic of community...what I do for others is returned to me, and in fact becomes something I have done for myself. I think it is quite likely that Harris lacked the empathy essential to living a mature life. I don't know if that was choice or affliction, but I saw its effects, and my mother had to live with them.

So while my mother knew what she was up against, she was also a young wife with two children in her care, and she needed more than her own inner voice. She needed help. So, her family came to the rescue. Shortly after her enlightening encounter with Harris, my grandfather Pop flew out to Palo Alto to be with her, and ended up providing her the voice she needed.

Grandfathers are often idolized, but I get to lay claim to one of the all-time greats. My mother had lost her own brilliant father, Richard Young, a neurologist and psychiatrist, to Parkinson's disease when he was but 50 and she was only 16. My grandmother Bami married Dale Clark who became our Pop about 10 years later, and our merged families got to spend incredible times together on the trips the two of them created for us. They were a wonderful match, and Pop treated all of his acquired grandchildren as though we were going to invent world peace.

The thing was, when Pop told us he thought we could invent world peace, we pretty well believed it too. Pop had been president of the Omaha Bank, he had been on the Union Pacific Railroad board, and was just about as many muckety-muck things as a person could be in Omaha. But he was also an avid collector of inspirational life stories, which he shared with us as kids, and shared with employees through the years if they were feeling down and out. He carried these things in pieces of paper in his pockets. I think the thing I loved best about him, though, was finding out that he had a weekly poker game with a group of guys who were...well... not members of the country club. By a long shot.

My grandmother insinuated that a few of these buddies had been convicts, but that may have been her opinion of anybody who couldn't get into the country club. Whoever they were, I always saw his poker pal parties as something to emulate. He understood that people are just people, and he went out of his way to know, love and be taught by as many as he could collect. He was a faithful, thoughtful, educated and compassionate guy. I have a friend who once described to me the Quaker concept of a "loving witness" who sees what is best in a person and translates that right back to them. I believe my Pop was a living example of such a witness and the precise guy anyone would want counsel from.

So my mother asked.

And he replied, "Daphne, everything everyone's telling you is true to one degree or another. The pluses are true, the minuses are true. You have to simply decide what is best for you and most of all, for your children.

"Consider what you want your family to be, and ignore the small things. What do you want the Big Things in life to look like? Decide what those things are, and let the little things work themselves out…and by the way, the things other people think are definitely little things.

"Here is the most helpful thing I can tell you: make your own decision, and then be deliberate."

Daphne took his advice to heart. She made her own decisions. She was deliberate. She was divorced, in custody of her children and back in Omaha before the year was out. And that experience made her a strong believer in making the best of the moments and the realities that she faced. But more than that, she believed in being decisive, in not wallowing in life's puddles, and she has expected the same of us.

In Daphne's world, life moves ahead. Thank God.

My mother's decision to break off her relationship with Harris, and to disconnect him from our lives, was accomplished with incredible grace and sensitivity toward us. As was my real dad's decision three years later to adopt Rich and me, treating us absolutely as his own for a lifetime.

And that began the life I really know as mine.

Together, my parents' love for each other created a life for all of us that was a textbook lesson in how parents design an environment so their children can flourish. I understood this only after I had children myself, and began to evaluate why certain things became very important to me as a mother. I had learned to reflexively protect my children not by standing close at all times, but by knowing where they would be safe, and pursuing or creating those settings. It seems very strange to me now that I didn't fully grasp the tremendous energy it took, over and over again, for my parents to know that all four of us were safe, that we had what we needed, that in so far as they could, they kept us from bad influence. And, all without appearing to do so.

After my parents married, they added my sister Anne and brother John to our party. Their expectations for all four of us were always high, but I actually don't remember ever thinking so. I didn't realize there were options. Both of my parents made it clear what our duties were, and punishments for failing them were enough to make an impact but they were never overly harsh. The hallmark of my parents is that they are extremely supportive.

My mom is the world's greatest audience. I still rely on hearing her opinion after some public appearance. This is not because I am starving for her attention, although I do enjoy it, as do my other family members. To put it more simply, we are show-offs and she is delighted to watch our shows. But the reason I am not starving for my mother's attention is because I know I always have it. I crave my mother's reactions about my work because she is a most genuine and descriptive supporter. She became the loving witness that Pop and others were for her—something I too strive to be.

I can know—I mean be absolutely certain—when I have given a mediocre performance in public. But if my mother was part of the audience, she'll call immediately to offer very specific detail on everything that was fabulous. Her positive commentary may only relate to my hairstyle and clothing; but it will be great to listen to nonetheless. And I will come away believing I was less catastrophic than previously imagined.

It is actually an ongoing gentle trick of my kids Justin and Annie to present my mom with something absolutely minimal they have created or done to see if they can get GrandMommy to do less than enthuse about their effort. To date, they have failed at this.

My favorite example was finding that my mom had prominently displayed a most bizarre plastic sculpture front and center in her kitchen. "Look at the mobile the kids made for me!" she exclaimed.

I stared at it for a minute, and then realized what it was. My dear children had opened a new board game, disconnected the playing pieces from that plastic frame they arrive adhered to, then put a string on the frame and gifted it to my mother as something they had made for her. This was their latest round of "how low can we go?" with GrandMommy.

I pointed this out. "Mom, I think they are just teasing you. They didn't actually make that—it's just the wrapping their new game pieces came in."

"What???" she questioned as she examined her new piece of art. Then she broke out laughing. "Honestly, I don't know who is smarter than those kids." She walked away giggling and marveling at her grandchildren. "Lulu, you are such a great mother to have raised such clever kids."

Suddenly I am riding the praise train merely for giving birth to these "artists." The woman is impossible to discourage.

As a further example of the true level of this responsiveness, my stepdaughter Kate loves to report how long it takes my mother to write a thank you note for a thank you note. Again, not kidding. If my mother does something wonderful for someone—and she will, often—they will most likely write her a note or give her a small gift in return. Whereupon, my mother will write them a note for the note. And it will be lovely. Not a soul can beat my mother at this game.

Simple Choices

With a mother like this, it was quite possible for my three siblings and I to grow up slightly overconfident. But here is where balance comes in. My mother's enthusiasm has a way of pushing her expectations on her children. She withdraws it when necessary. There is no happy talk from my mom when one of us is obviously giving less or doing less than she believes we are capable. Genuine effort gets the regular world-class praise response. Not trying? Purposefully breaking the rules? Moping? (My mother still uses this word.) Not Good. A silent opprobrium from the world's happiest cheerleader is a sentence you don't want.

And to further the balanced upbringing, my father requires an altogether more substantive return for his expectations.

My sister and I were both lucky enough to ride horses competitively from a very young age until after we were married. My father's immediate response when told we'd won a competition was, "How many in the class?"

Dad needs to know his enthusiasm is warranted. If any of his children manage to win in a truly competitive challenge, however, he is impressed and says so. He won't write us a note, but he is pleased nonetheless.

My mom and dad are a perfect team. The only sure way to really piss off my parents is to do one of two things: Don't try, or complain. They just don't get that. They expect us to work hard, do well, do good, be well, live happy.

If we are unhappy, they are sympathetic, they are there for us. For about as long as they feel we need to get on with it.

And after that interval they impose their life lessons learned. They've known difficult circumstances. They understand life can be rough. They also know that we have been graced with family support, and with the intellectual capacity to figure these things out, and to resume our work in the world. They expect us to do that, and so we try.

It's been a good way to approach life.

Chapter Six
Choosing an Adult Path

I thank God every day that my parents are thorough and committed adults. Without knowing I had done so, I absorbed their happy example and have made sort of a study-in-hindsight about what it was they did that gave me the confidence and the ability to pursue my life and purpose.

And I'd like to pass that along. Not because I recommend what I learned as a perfect recipe—I don't believe in such a thing. But I do believe that parents ought to exercise a simple, deliberate intention for their children to be useful to the world, according to their own gifts. A commitment to that principle doesn't make raising children any easier. But building on that foundation helps parents make sense of the job.

Everyone wants children to be happy. Of course. But happy is an outcome of something. It's a condition, not an end.

I want my children to be of service; because that is why I think they—and every child—arrived here in the first place. I want all children to be trained to contribute to the community they find themselves in, whether that community is simply the person they happen to be sitting next to or in a much larger, shared community. I want them to believe that is their responsibility, and to take it upon their shoulders. I want them to know themselves well enough to be free to rise up out of themselves and to help, assist, witness and love other people. Because commitment to people and causes beyond ourselves is what makes people thrive.

I believe that every parent's job is to make those little shoulders ready and willing.

Here is the deal about shepherding children as I see it: Whatever you do when you are on your own or away from the eyes and ears of children is up to you. But where your children or children under your influence are concerned, be an adult. By this I mean be comfortable with the wisdom and maturity you've developed. Sometimes that means playing and sharing the joy in your heart with children as though you share their age, other times it means offering a solid barrier against danger or dangerous behavior that only an adult would recognize.

All children learn what they know about themselves and those around them from the example of their parents and caregivers. And they learn at the level of maturity their parents portray. I have no idea what behaviors my parents engaged in when their children were not around. I suspect that had they been way too interesting, we would have known that. But what I observed at home on a daily and repetitive basis was two people who were committed to each other and to their work in the world. One piece of their work was their four children, and we were a big piece. But we didn't trump all. We were part of a long history of family members who arrived on the scene to grow up and offer ourselves to the communities and individuals we thought we could influence toward a greater good. And that is an undeniable privilege that has nothing to do with wealth, status or the unpredictable forces of life.

The fact is, parents have a choice about how this goes. Adults can approach their role in children's lives in a number of ways…everything from the first extreme of believing that they do have and should have control over a child's most intimate decisions from birth to graduation from college and beyond. Or, adults can adopt the opposite extreme, choosing to sit back and let life buffet the kids around, pretending to have no power to exercise on their behalf, allowing lots of drama with little explanation, reasoning or planning for future consequences.

Truly, I have to say I am thoroughly amazed at the number of people who choose the latter. Far too many people choose to be parents when they seem unwilling to assert any control or organizing principle over their own lives. They treat their children as they treat everyone, as players in a drama that revolves around them. It is infantile, but prevalent, and I am acutely sensitive to it because my mother saved me from being raised in that environment.

As with most things, act to avoid either extreme; it is fundamentally important that parents get this right. Kids are stuck with whom they get as parents. And if they've got you, your role as a parent is just too much of an honor, too critical to the development of the life that follows you, for you to allow yourself the excesses of behavior that make a child's world insecure. Your first priority must always be that whatever you choose to do, however you choose to live, you must create within that life a place of safety, security and meaning for your children. And you can help to build that by offering your children a lens through which to view life events.

In order to be of great service to the people around them, and to the world in general, children must learn to see and believe in their inherent value. They must learn to trust who they are and what they are drawn to. And they must see the qualities they possess as tools that can be developed in order to achieve a much larger end.

It seems incredibly trite to suggest (as some advice to parents does) that parenting can be reduced to "Three Easy Steps!" because it cannot be. Instead, let me offer three rules I learned at home that offer a path to raising children to love themselves and make their individual lives a benefit to their communities. For me, these three rules have been a most beautiful trio of guideposts.

Guidepost #1: All parents are sacred to their children because children see themselves as reflections of their parents. Support and promote this at all times.

Guidepost #2: See your children for who they are, and allow them to develop the gifts that are unique to them. They have them for a reason.

Guidepost #3: Children need to see their lives and their work in a sacred context. So do you.

Chapter 7

Guidepost One

The dictionary definition of "sacred" includes the words "dedicated," "devoted," "worthy," "holy" and "valued." Those words are perfect descriptors of what parents should aspire to be, and they certainly reflect the way our children see us, regardless of how well we meet the aspiration.

Guidepost #1: All parents are sacred to their children; children see themselves as reflections of their parents. Support and promote this at all times.

In order to fully appreciate my commitment to this first rule, know that, like Daphne, I had a starter marriage. Mine was in fact a happy marriage to a tremendous person, and we were blessed with two incredible children. It did not end as dramatically as my mother's.

My first marriage ceased to work at a certain point. And it didn't work for reasons intimately understood only by the two of us who created it. What I will tell you is that even in the legal-no-fault divorce state of Arizona, the end of our marriage was absolutely my fault, and absolutely his. That fact and our mutual willingness to acknowledge it early and often, allowed us to remain a family to this day. We ended our marriage; we didn't end our relationship or our responsibility to parent our beautiful children together.

After my first husband and I had both remarried to wonderful people, we all four chose to attend counseling in order to become the best possible parents we could be to our children. I know, yikes! But we were all blessed to be married to people who believe that raising children well is Job One.

Adding to the richness of my family is the fact that my husband, John Keegan, was married for over 20 years to one of the people I admire most in the world, my stepchildren's mother, Mary Keegan. Mary and John also had a happy marriage before it ended, and are fabulous parents to their three beautiful children. They made a conscious choice that the end of their marriage would not be the end of their relationship or their commitment to a shared family.

That may seem just a little too nice, and over the years we have been told we must be making this up. We aren't.

First of all, not only is all of this true, it has allowed us to abide by Guidepost #1. We support our children by loving exactly who they are. And children are who their parents are. Therefore, we love, respect and speak well of our children's other parents.

Second, you may need to get out more, because I have discovered that many families have this happy kind of consolidation going on. It discourages me that it isn't the norm, and that people seem to get so much apparent joy out of holding on to their anger and hurt for decades. I think that is richly deserving of being ignored. Do the world a favor... don't encourage your friends to stay angry about their troubled, ending or ended relationships by supporting trash talk about ex-spouses if there are children involved. Suggest they move on, and never get sucked into conversations that disparage a child's parent when the children are there to hear it. Ever.

But finally, and on the more difficult side, this happy family we have now was really, really difficult at first and very hard won. Did I say really? Because, really, it was.

Being convinced that divorce occurred because the ex-partner was an absolute idiot/schmuck/ogre is a necessary step in dissolving a bond that started out as something both legal and sacred. It is not something that can ever be taken lightly; one does not end a marriage on a whim. Or if they do, they are not people I have ever met.

So in order to understand or rationalize why divorce is the only option, people naturally catalogue the faults that lead to the reasons. And no doubt there are good reasons. But the danger lies in believing that the behaviors that caused the decision to divorce should lead to a complete end of the relationship. Or the danger becomes encouraging others (*especially children*) to believe that a lousy relationship is the only kind of relationship the other partner is capable of having.

That is usually not true.

And here I will resort to some family wisdom yet again. My mother's father was a well-known psychiatrist and neurologist who worked with mental illness, and his brother, my great uncle Bobby, was a psychologist who worked with mental health. Well, he worked to help people attain it. This expanse of interests and career paths fascinated me and I have always wanted to understand what got discussed at dinner when they were growing up, but alas, I never got to know these men.

What I did get to know was a lot of Bobby's thinking, because he was a prolific writer who got to live longer than my grandfather. And one of the most useful things I ever learned was Bobby's view on human behavior. Without trying to make it prettier than it is, because none of us is that pretty, Bobby's philosophy was the following: Each of us is comprised of roughly 25 percent bullshit. And from time to time, we either act with 100 percent of our 25 percent, or we are only willing to see the 25 percent of somebody else.

Thanks to Uncle Bobby, I believe that the period of time when you are getting divorced is a 25 percent kind of time. You're about 100 percent deep in it.

Here is some really caring advice for those of you who are hanging on to whatever reasons caused you to end a marriage: Get over yourself. It was your fault, too. And if you have children, the only way you can possibly raise them well, whether or not you find a way to raise the children in an ongoing but separate partnership, is to find a way back to loving the person who brought this child into the family with you. The love and respect will be there. Look for it, and remember it; make it real, make it work.

I have had many, many people over the years tell me that they don't understand how, if I can love my first husband still, I could ever have allowed our marriage to end. This is a common fishing expedition, and can be a tempting moment. It could be a perfect opening to share a litany of former-spouse horrors. Resist. Say you don't know. Say life is mysterious, but you and your former spouse are both very happy now, and you are so grateful that you still have a close relationship.

But since inquiring minds do want to know...try oversharing some fun facts like I'm going to do right here. Share how you spend holidays and select vacation times all together with former spouses and in-laws as a family. Relay stories about the times you care for children from your spouse's new marriage. Include details such as how your former mother-in-law is friends with your stepdaughter's father-in-law, or how you and your husband's first wife convinced your future son-in-law to join you all in a board game of "Family Therapy" the first time he met all of you. It will freak them out and they won't ask again. It will also make the point that you are a real live family with tribal stories like any great family has.

I could actually write for some time on the shape of our family and how it works. And I would do that except my daughters are considering the same writing from their perspective, and I would rather read about our lives through their words than my own. Those women, who wrote the foreword for this book, are gifted writers and I look forward to it.

What I will say is that we have had a most amazing life-as-family together, and that life was originally grounded in a commitment to Guidepost #1. You cannot bluff your kids on what you think of their other parents; they know. So in order to think well of each other, we had to get to a place where we genuinely appreciated each other...either again or for the first time in the case of new parties on the scene. And like everything that must be done well, it took some practice.

I can tell you that I vividly remember my first shouting match with the woman who would become my children's stepmother. It was early in her relationship with my former husband, but far enough along that she had become a steady presence in my children's lives.

I know that we were on the phone.

What I don't remember is what we were arguing about, or specifically what we were saying. What I do remember is that I was furious, so was she, and we were deeply into exercising our respective 25 percents. As it happens, we were both having this phone call within earshot of our partners, who obviously could not hear the full conversation. But we would find out later that each man was urging the same thing: "You really need to put down the phone."

And both of us were giving our partners the universal female body language for "What? Put down the phone? I am just getting started here." It's a look.

The fact is that very few people can or will agree to go toe-to-toe with me in an argument. I kind of like arguing; I may do it for sport occasionally. I know I have done it often enough to get really good at it. And for the first time in my life, my black belt in blather was having zero effect on this woman. None. In fact, the better I got, the better she got. Horrendous. Eventually, we wore each other down without either of us giving an inch, and hung up.

I don't know what Kathleen did in the moments that followed, but I turned away from the phone and spent about five straight minutes on a sportscaster-style replay of the bout for my husband. Followed by about 30 seconds of silence.

And ending with this: "I *really* like her!"

From that conversation on, I saw that this woman could deploy herself in defense of my children, and I knew that she would. And I was right; Kathleen is a strong, beautiful woman who has been a phenomenal mother to my children. I know that Justin and Annie are better people for having grown up with Kathleen in our lives.

Abiding by Guidepost #1 is never easy. Not in a case of divorce and not in a family that remains intact. Because at some juncture, we are all married to idiots; even our spouses. Sometimes it is damn hard not to say so when your kids are in the room. But it matters enormously. Children absolutely identify their value with the value of their parents. You can wish that fact away, but it is true. And it is true even when a child's parent is genuinely dishonorable.

So every time you accost your child with a criticism of his or her parent, you are accusing them of the same. It's one of those excesses that feels good at the time, but poisons the child in the long run. Resist and avoid doing this with all your might. And, if you do give in to this sort of blashphemy, apologize to the child as well as to the other parent.

Unless you share children with somebody who is genuinely harmful or dangerous, constantly expressing your love and support for your child's parent(s) is absolutely essential. If you find yourself in the horrible situation of having a dangerous partner as a co-parent, you of course cannot entrust your child to their care (and that is the reason for the court system—you can and should get a legal judgment to enforce against such danger), but neither must you degrade that person. It is best to honestly tell the child that the parent has such problems that he or she is overwhelmed by them and cannot be the good person they were meant to be. Keep in mind that the child needs to find their own internal value in being tied to this person. If you share the concepts of hope and faith with a child who is in this situation, the two of you can either join to pray for or think well of this important, yet hurting, soul. I think of my mother and the wonderful stories she told me about how Harris was a really smart, really gifted man who had problems. But he loved me. That's all I knew. It was enough.

Likewise, if there is no willingness on other sides of the family to set all the vitriol aside, a parent will not be able to accomplish the one happy family thing alone. And this is very difficult. But don't be tempted to get even or to give up; believe that there is hope for the best outcome and you play an important role in such hope. The fact that others can't or won't find their way to forgiveness and a supportive relationship should not be an excuse for you to denigrate your child's family.

So I hope other parents can keep positive even in these really trying situations…you never know, sometimes miracles happen! And at a minimum, the goal is for the child to learn that there is good in everybody. Mostly, in the child.

If you are in a family that has always been just the one family, that's very cool. For you, the habit of expressing support for each other as parents should come easier; but it is still a necessary discipline. Every now and then, try to count how many times in a day your children hear you say something absolutely supportive of your partner and the other people—especially adults—who are helping to shape their lives.

If you are raising children in a blended or separate family, it's more of a challenge because there are more people, more chances to communicate, more logistics, but the rewards for this kind of endurance are also greater. Divorce is a terrible experience for children. It is true that nothing that happens afterward can ever undo the hurt or erase the memory of it. But dealing with it in an honest and forthright manner offers children an opportunity to expand the view of their lives rather than to believe the experience was only negative.

All of us need help navigating transitions like this, and I recommend learning about the ACE consortium. ACE offers a clear analysis for why parents must not expose children to unnecessary pain, as well as specific suggestions for how to avoid doing so. We can always learn ways to get better.

I remember sitting with Annie when she was about 6 years old, drawing a heart, then a heart cleft in two that we made whole again but larger by "coloring it back together." I told Annie that the people who were capable of the most happiness in the world were people who had broken hearts, but had the courage to mend them again. Their hearts just get bigger and bigger, and those people can love more and more. I believe in that.

Life is full of opportunities to be hurt, and families can be the source of much of it - if we allow that. But working through what is difficult to arrive at a place where children understand that they are the reason for the concentrated effort to be a solid, loving family...that will keep their sense of personal worth and value intact. They will be able to be who they were made to be—with confidence.

My life blessed me with experience in divorce first as a child, and then as a mother. In both cases, Guidepost #1 was honored, and I believe that is what created our beautiful... or "epic", to borrow from my daughters... family.

I love my children's parents, all of them. And when I see my children or grandchildren mirror physical or behavioral aspects of their parents, I rejoice in that just as much as any mother who watches the life cycle carried on through those they love. Example: I cannot fathom a life where I could not take joy in small, beautiful things like the crooked baby finger that my grandson inherited from his grandmother Mary, my husband's first wife. But more than that little finger, he shares her generosity of spirit that I have also been privileged to know and love. And he hears that from me and from his grandfather. We celebrate that together as any family should.

And my children hear a steady stream of genuine support and admiration from me and from my husband for their father. It is easy to do this, as their father is a tremendous community developer and philanthropist, but they also hear from us that we admire those personal things that resemble their dad...they possess his work ethic, his intelligence, and in my daughter's case, an obsession with lists! It is all lovely to see, and I am eternally grateful that our family has adopted the Daphne-esque habit of saying so right out loud.

Our children have been fed the same steady diet of family experiences and family stories that I grew up with. Those stories spring from love for each other, respect for the work of our shared families, and in the hope that our children will develop their own gifts and contribute to the world as their ancestors have.

Whatever the shape of a family...be it linked by blood, marriage or merely by commitment to each other...children must easily see how they fit. And it is up to their parents and caretaker partners to build a framework that beautifully accommodates them, everybody they love and everybody who loves them.

It's a puzzle well worth putting together.

Chapter Eight

Guidepost Two

***

The art form of excellent parenting is to develop an eye for the gifts a child has and their willingness to develop those, even before anyone has any idea where the child's life will take them.

> *Guidepost #2: See your children for who they are, and allow them to develop the gifts that are unique to them. They have them for a reason.*

The first job parents have is to lay a sure foundation for our children. Children must be secure; they must understand they are loved; they are safe; they are important. In addition though, they must be taught to use the specific physical and intellectual gifts they were given in a way that will keep them challenged and able to act on the purpose they determine is theirs. That means adults must pay attention to their health, to their activities and especially to their education.

In order to do this all of this well, parents must find a way to set themselves and their needs, fears and shortcomings aside. And that is easier said than done. There is just no way to be a parent without trying – at one time or another - to impose our version of a perfect life on our children. When parents feel they have lived a pretty happy and productive life, they may be tempted to create another version of themselves, or to create a Mini-Me. Or worse, parents may sense that somehow they missed out on something, and usurp a child to attempt a Better-Me.

Instead, focus on helping a child to develop the skills that they will need in order to be great contributors. But remember that this child will get to make the ultimate decision about how to deploy all this excellence he or she is being helped to create.

Let's face it; they really are brats that way.

But when they are your brats, you are completely, soulfully, vibrantly in love with them. So your job as a parent is not to design exactly who your child will become, but to help your children understand their unique and important place in the world, in whatever way your family understands that. If you haven't had the blessing and grace of a family that taught you that we are here for a purpose, read about others who do. Copy their actions and their words. Read stories about great causes and talk about the heroes and heroines of those causes with your children.

Without a doubt, life gives models of character and behavior that provide amazing examples of the traits children can emulate—the same traits all adults should be striving to emulate. And the people who exemplify those things are heroic. They inspire.

Stories of heroic behavior ought to be staples in every child's life from a very early age. There are so many wonderful books about great figures in history, and those stories help children to formulate an understanding of what service out of love for others looks like.

My careers gave me the very precious opportunity to introduce historic figures to my children, but also to introduce them to living heroes who have literally changed the world for the better. My children have had the honor of meeting several of my colleagues whose work with schools and families has improved the trajectory of millions of lives. And always on this list is Senator John McCain, as he was the first politician I ever volunteered for in 1986 after hearing him speak at a community forum during his first run for the U.S. Senate.

Senator McCain became a mentor to me years later when I was in the Arizona state legislature, then expanded that role when I decided to run for state school superintendent. As I was sitting in my campaign office after deciding to run for the superintendent post in the spring of 1994, I got a call from senator McCain. You should know that conversations with this Senator were and are direct.

Without knowing the caller, I picked up the telephone and said, "Hello."

"You are going to run for superintendent," his familiar voice was clear.

"Yes, sir."

"Do you have a chairman yet?"

"No."

"Well now you do, if you want one."

I was speechless. But he wasn't.

"And Lisa?"

"Yes?"

"Don't lose."

That was it. I have believed over the years, and through both of his presidential campaigns that I was honored to work on, that the fear of disappointing John McCain has motivated me far more than most things. He is a walking inspiration to me and our children learned his story early in their lives from me.

But through my relationship working with Senator McCain, our children also grew to understand that deep respect does not preclude disagreement. They learned that *disagreement* does not mean *dislike*. Teaching children about heroes is about helping them understand that everyone has the power to exceed themselves…to be bigger by offering leadership in order to help everybody else. And that doesn't always mean the same thing as just being someone who is fun to hang out with.

There is plenty of heroic behavior out there, found in all kinds of people. Make sure children know about it, and help them identify these heroic traits in themselves. It is important to tell children what is heroic and wonderful about them. Be specific and honest; kids have very finely tuned bullshit sensors. There are a couple of tools I rely on to get past any bullshit: ink, a pen, paper, electricity, pixels, screens. I write to my children.

It is one thing to tell a child something, but it is entirely different when they get a chance to read about themselves. To hold a letter in their hands makes the fact that they are loved even more tangible.

Writing to children about what makes them unique forces a person to really think through that from time to time. It's a great way to share your thoughts with them, and it lasts. Copies of letters serve as lasting reminders, too. For one thing, when children are making you crazy there will be written proof that at one point in time you saw and recorded their value.

I write most often to Annie and Justin, because they are my primary responsibility. With my stepchildren, I am playing secondary support on a really strong team of parents. But I inflict my thoughts on all of the children, and now children in-law, at least occasionally. As I wrote early in this book, I am a big believer in the power of words.

I hesitated to share the very personal writing that has been part of my life with my children, but I think it is right to do that now. Because I have worked in the public eye, I place a high value on my privacy, so I'm sharing these letters out of a belief that these examples may inspire others to memorialize the best of what they see in their children through writing to them. Because these are private letters, I made sure that both Justin and Annie allowed me to print them.

This first set of letters was written to both children when they were about 17 and close to finishing high school. I was feeling their imminent departure and these letters reflect the dozens of notes and letters I wrote to both of them over the years.

Guidepost Two

Dear Justin,

You know how proud of you I am by now, I hope. And it is a funny and wonderful thing to be not just proud of you as I was when you were little... but now proud to watch you as a friend, a respected part of the community we share, and more than ever, a person whose hopes and dreams are his own.

To begin with, I was proud of you for the little things. Little miracles, to me. I was proud when you smiled, when you walked, when you talked. Very proud when you were funny...which has never ceased...proud when it became obvious very early on you were somebody others trusted and gravitated to. Really proud when you first went to school and I could see you were no ordinary intellect. And amazingly proud and relieved when you and Annie both settled into your lives in two houses with two families—hopefully and thankfully really one big family.

I was so proud of your first communion...because I think I knew even then that your journey with God would be so intensely personal, that being your Sunday school teacher and sharing the amazing story of communion with you would be a very rare time when you and I would "share" one set of information on this beautiful topic. That may sound odd, but as your mother, I was your teacher then. And as you know, I believe with all my heart that God sends us to the parents we need, and he sends parents the children they can teach...and reach. And I wanted you to understand my own awe of communion, and the power I believe its existence gives our lives. I wanted its power in your life...to guard your life, to keep you.

And that may be as good a working metaphor that I have for explaining life as your mom and your biggest fan.

You know intense love. And you know the joy of showing a loved one what is a wonder in your own life...of wanting to share it, to have the joy of that event or experience or thought influencing the life of your loved one as it does you. You know, showing Disneyland to somebody! Only more so....

Well, as your mother I have known the greatest joy imaginable when you and I both thought something was funny when you were a baby, when we agree on philosophy or political theory now, or when we are discovering new countries and cultures together. I don't know why that is so wonderful, but it is absolute joy. And as you know, I believe that kind of intense happiness in the joy and discovery of a loved one...is clear evidence of God's love for us.

Simple Choices

So I know you wonder why your dad and I seek in ways both subtle and annoyingly obvious to influence your life in matters such as faith, friends, your life path, your music, sports, colleges...and the best answer I can find is that we are seeking a communion with you. A sharing of the best of life that we have known, and a desire for you to experience that as well.

But the fact is that you will experience a life we can never know. There will continue to be those wonderful moments of shared experience and joy—and as your parents we will seek those more often than you will, no doubt—but this is really the juncture where you declare your independent path.

It requires an act of the greatest faith to simply let you experience your life and your God as He has given you to understand your life...and Him. I can't know or understand how that is for you, and that fact is both lonely and awesome (in the actual sense of the word). I can only imagine from your actions how strongly your life pulls you to its service. I can relate to that only from my own experience, but know it is unique to you. I am truly awed by watching you.

And I trust you. Your actions have taught us that we can and should trust you, that you are ready for your life.

One thing that makes you ready is your foundation in an amazing family. It is the most incredible gift to know one has a "home base" of family and friends who see us not only as we are, but as we want to be. Justin, nobody has ever been loved by more people. It is just a part of you, this incredible unwieldy family that adores you. I thank God for that gift to you every day.

I love you, Justin. And I will always be thankful that God thought enough of me, to send you. You bring incredible gifts to the world. Always have the faith and courage to use them.

You will know how.

Love, Mommy

And then to Annie three years later:

My Beautiful Annie is 17.

Just over 17 years ago, I first saw you. Your tiny face was front and center on an ultrasound at about five months, and I looked at that constantly until you were born, amazed that I would feel such recognition from the first time I saw you. So I have always known you somehow.

When you were finally born, your arrival telegraphed your character. It wasn't so much that you were late...it was more that you wanted to be scheduled for, easily anticipated, something on a daily to-do list. Your preference for order and scheduled on-time arrivals was clear. What a sense of humor God has that He sent you to me ☺*!*

So the doctor scheduled for you to be "induced" at about 1 in the afternoon on October 10. And arrive efficiently you did, about 5 hours later. What I remember most was how calm and friendly the atmosphere was while we waited for you.

So finally in the evening, there was Annie all the sudden!! A real live GIRL! Meme and GrandMommy just stared at you...and you stared back. I have never seen, nor do I expect to see, a baby hold the gaze of everybody she met. It was amazing and a little unnerving, actually. It seemed you were expecting us to do something, or at least try to impress you! Most babies will turn away first, put their chin down, and look shyly back. Not Annie. You kept this up for months, and I wondered if you were trying to memorize people and figure how they would play in your life somehow.

As you got a few months older and started to smile, you were a bit stingy with the giggle games. Usually, you would still just hold our eyes with this expectant gaze...neither smiling or frowning...just searching. You actually still do it! I think it is an ability born of confidence, which seems to be a happy part of your nature. You meet the world on its terms, neither trying to enchant it to you with charm (which you have in abundance), nor repelling it or rejecting it by refusing its gaze. You are one of the most present people I know.

I have been completely humbled to be your mother, because you know I believe God sends us the children that need us. You have SO many gifts, that I think they just tumble to the fore in you, and you are just madly impatient to DO YOUR SERVICE!!! I thought so often how little you cared for being very young. It was a passage you just seemed to have little love for. You need to

Simple Choices

be doing something meaningful in your eyes, and there are seemingly fewer options when you are four. That seemed very obvious to you. I have felt that it has been...and is...part of my role to keep you calm and try to relax you into the fact that sometimes the only way to get to your service is to wait, and listen. To be ready, but not in pursuit, and not dismissive of the daily acts of everyday living that can feel like smaller service...but matter so very much.

You are such a treasure to your friends and family, honey. I have just never met anybody who gets to know you who does not go out of their way to tell me how much they love Annie Graham. Never just Annie...always Annie Graham. Your thoughtfulness and caring for people is such an easy, constant part of you...it makes me very proud to watch you. You have chosen to be not just a friend, but in many ways a caretaker to your friends, a leader for them. Your acceptance of the fact that your life has been blessed and therefore you owe a deeper level of service is just palpable. Not a burden, but a happy fact for you, I think.

When I worry for you, it is most because you set such high standards for yourself, and always have. Nobody's critique of you will ever match your own, and I want to make sure that is also true for your ability to acknowledge how wonderful you are...and how much you try to fit into your life. You will need to make peace with the constant of a full plate. It will wait for you... and you will need to make space for recharging. Either through watching the very intellectual likes of "America's Top Model" and "Lost" or YouTube, or sleeping!!! Annie will always need to give Annie a break.

What an amazing moment in your life. You have established such a wonderful role for yourself at Xavier, in your sports and leadership there... and with such wonderful friends. And now you get to look to the next chapter. Hopefully at Stanford, which I believe is a perfect place for you. Or maybe life has another option in store for you...whatever it is, you will be an integral part of that community just as you have been in all your life's villages!!

I could never tell you how proud of you I am, nor how much it means to simply hear your voice, know you are happily busy, or especially spend time with you. It is wonderful simply to watch your life unfold...or more aptly, to watch you create your life.

I love you so much. Happy Birthday, Beautiful Annie.
Love, Mommy

Guidepost Two

I have years' worth of these letters and notes to my children and theirs to me tucked away in drawers and files all over the house. I would like to tell you that I have them neatly arranged in chronological order and in a single notebook where they can be easily accessed. But that is not true, and isn't necessary.

What I think matters so much about this kind of writing to a child is that it allows parents to be quite specific about what it is the child brings to the world that is uniquely theirs. It's hard to work that kind of description into everyday conversation, and children do need to develop a strong story line about who they are and what they do well. A parent's words can help a lot. And developing a habit of writing these things down can make it much easier to stay connected when the child is away. I am sure that raising children in two houses as we did made writing essential in order to stay connected from very early on. But I found over the years that it also gave me a voice I rarely used on a day-to-day, "let's get things done" basis. It's hard to talk to your child about their beautiful gifts when they are searching for lost backpacks and homework five minutes before they are supposed to be at school.

As they learn more about the world and their place in it, children will rely more and more on a reflexive belief about themselves. Whatever it is they were told about who they are, the value of who they are, and how they might use their talents, is going to show up in their behavior as adults. Hopefully, whether through writing or in quiet conversations, they will have heard from a parent, or another loving witness, what amazing gifts they possess.

When it is time for children to leave home and family and to discover the very intimate details of their own lives, be ready to be surprised and enthusiastic. They are unleashing their very own superpowers. Try to remember they are listening to a calling not meant for you. And this goes for life orientation as well as for work; hope for your children to be heroic in their lives.

Simple Choices

I think what is heroic about a life is the ability to live it honestly and with enthusiasm. I don't think that people are made the way they are by accident. While I absolutely accept the horrendous and chance impact of disease or disorder...I don't accept that the basic mystery of who a person is, is anything short of divinely inspired.

Period.

I frankly could not do the work that I do on behalf of choice in education if I did not believe so strongly in everyone's responsibility to see and develop young people just as they are. I believe that we are all different, that our talents are different—and that there is great intention in that scenario. The world needs all of us.

So it is alarming to me the degree to which our society has yet to come to grips with the various superpowers the Creator gives us. People differ in lots of ways...in their intellect, in their physical prowess, in their ethnicity, in their sexual nature. And for every one of those "differences," defined as that which goes against the norm in a particular culture, humanity has historically assigned some unfavorable and mythical explanation that we have gradually grown past. And let me emphasize "gradually" here.

So here is something I believe, and something I hold as both certain and sacred: The essence of a person exists inherently, expressly created for a purpose only one individual will truly understand. And given the proper encouragement, security, love and skills, the individual will develop their essence honestly, productively and according to the gifts they have been given.

So if parents get it right, and if schools enhance this good start, then children get to be who they were made to be.

Which means if you are somebody's parent, caregiver, relative, teacher or friend your responsibility to them doesn't change the first time a child reveals something about themselves that you did not know existed, or you had not acknowledged, or maybe something is revealed that you feel uncomfortable with. All of this means your role as an important player in the life of a child just got real, because these moments are not about you.

Here is my personal example: My Annie began dating a beautiful young woman who she met during her freshman year at Stanford, and she was very uneasy about sharing this particular piece of her identity with all of us in her family. Annie knew that we were enthusiastic about people being free to be whoever they truly are, as she has a wonderful uncle who married his partner, now husband and additional uncle, years ago. And one of Annie's cousins is a lesbian who married her beautiful wife at a wonderful family wedding the summer before Annie came out to us. She knew she had supportive family.

But it's just difficult. I wish it were not.

While I know that each of us is designed to be just as we are, the fact that a minority of us are created lesbian, gay, bisexual or transgender, means these members of our communities live with a de facto "markedness", to borrow a term from my linguistics background. To try and put this simply, linguistic theory explains that humans comprehend any concept we consider primary as an "unmarked" version of the concept, the "default" version. Any time we need to adapt the concept slightly, it must be "marked" with the addition of a prefix, a tense marker, or some other alteration. The theory is not so much about grammar as it is about how our brains manage meaning. We expect our own normative concepts, which are easier for us to process. And we create those norms from what we see most often, what we are used to, what we have learned is just "the way that it is".

Even when it really isn't. As in intimate relationships. Whatever in our lives is not the norm for us – be it ethnicity, handedness, intellectual capacity, sexual orientation, social status, or a host of other things – is "marked" in our minds as a variant expression. All of us carry what others see as variant expressions and one of those will usually be the "superpower" variant that leads to our purpose. Normative behaviors rarely change the world. But they don't threaten it, either.

And that is what makes being honest about the blessings of an LGBT orientation difficult. It is not yet considered a happy variant by everybody, even though it is every bit as predictable in society as left-handedness. Where being left-handed is a variant, we attribute no real mythology to it. (Unless you are left-handed like my husband in which case your mythology is that you are just smarter than everybody else.)

Being a member or ally of the LGBT community makes you fully aware of other people's unflattering mythology. Some of that is fear ironically born of religious training, a fact I nearly cannot comprehend. The loving God I understand does not censor his own creation. I hope that in my lifetime we will reach a point where young people like my Annie do not need to wonder if the love that sustains them will be treated as less than the wondrous miracle that any true love is.

When Annie and I first spoke to each other about this, I was visiting her at Stanford and we sat in a Greek restaurant and we talked and we cried and we told each other "you're wonderful." I was so proud of her for living as she was created to live, and I knew that getting to the point she could share this must have cost her. As my mother explained later when we were discussing Annie's relationship, Mom sensed Annie's loss of not feeling able to share the joy of falling in love as it happened. She said, "Annie had this wonderful news, and she couldn't simply take for granted that we would all be excited."

I wished that Annie's story about meeting and falling in love with a girl who grew up and lived just blocks away from Annie all these years could be as easy to tell as any young love story. Annie's particular story was very romantic. The difficulty is with people who look past the love in order to focus on the gender match as a contrast to gender duality—when either kind of relationship is perfectly suited for true and intimate love. I believe all loving relationships that seek us out and transform our lives for the better are blessed by a loving Creator.

So I reminded Annie of everything I had been telling her over the years about who she was from the moment I met her. She is loving, she is present for people, she is brilliant, she is strong, she has a purpose. I could see that part of her life's purpose would be to accept herself with such confidence and peace that she would inspire others to accept themselves and those around them in the same way. I hoped that I had said all of these things enough over the years to convince her that she was easily strong enough to openly embrace everything about who I see as Beautiful Annie.

After I left her that day to fly across the country, I sat in the airport and wrote an email to her, and a while later she wrote back, and this went on for a while. I was so happy that for us, writing to each other was a reflexive habit, and something we could call on to offer support to each other.

I want to share some of those email letters with you, because as precious and personal as they are to me and to Annie, we both think they have great power for families who are walking this less trodden and lovely path. Annie started this by publishing pieces of the letters in her *Stanford Daily* newspaper articles. So I blame her…for discovering that the words she and I shared were very helpful to others.

On Oct 23, 2011, at 9:06 PM, Lgkeegan wrote:

Subject Line: So the Happiest Part of a Very Happy Day…

…is to finally hear you say that you are in a relationship. I am sure the scary part of planning how you let people into this part of your life is to deal with the gender issue rather than the fact of the relationship itself.

Which is why I told you I was so happy to hear you say you are dating Erica, and to put it just like that.

Romantic relationships are pure risk, full stop. You can have all sorts of impersonal connections to people involving various late nights and close physical contact. And according to the Grumpy Old Codger News that parents read, that is what you kids do these days.

But I always wanted to hear you say that you had decided to risk this kind of relationship, and though we have not known Erica all that long, we love her and I can certainly see why the two of you work. You may not realize what a joy it is to hear that somebody you respect obviously sees all the wonder of the daughter you love.

I love you, Annie. And I hope that you and Erica can create more focus on pure joy in the relationship and the beauty of your lives than on having to worry about how to frame this for others.

The easiest thing for those who love you to believe in is your happiness.

And bringing this back around to me (obviously, and fairly late in a long message, actually) you added enormously to my own happiness today.

Much love to you and God bless, sweetie. The One who sent you here must also be so proud that you are choosing the honest life. There is just no other way to do the service you were sent for.

Be happy.

XXXXOOOO

Mommy

On Oct 24, 2011, at 2:41 PM, Annie Graham <aegraham> wrote:

Mom…!

Those words were very helpful. I love you and thank you and usually I'm the best and most witty and most fun and most superlative writer ever, but I can't find the words to respond adequately. So I'll say this: I've talked to a few people about how they did this (the ol' telling of the parents) because it's always an interesting story and reaction. I was talking to some really close friends (gay ladies, also, which is important to their reaction) last night and they were tearing up a peculiar 'tearing up' of the joy of disbelief because the things you said were just...so...not hurtful at all and really nice and helpful (see my loss for words here?).

Every time someone "reacts" well, or says really nice things, especially a parent, people cling to that and feel like this is okay and this is a viable thing and this can be good for the world, just like any good relationship can.

So thank you. And for focusing on the fact that I'm just livin' my life and am now trying to be in a relationship, which is just as hard for everyone, and that you can respect the person I've chosen for this particular journey (while enduring and laughing at potential confusion, throat-clearing, ho-humming, and general discontent from the peanut gallery).

I love you and John and feel loved and thank you. And also, go write some book.

Love,

Annie

On Oct 24, 2011, at 2:08 PM, Lgkeegan wrote:

I am so so glad. And you and Erica both need to be ready for others to be genuinely happy for you. John and I have already had a number of conversations about how relieved and happy we are.

You are such a private person, which is a good thing, that we have not known if you were feeling like you were ready to share your life. And at some point, well, we just worried you were going to either find a dysfunctional person to be with, or be on the Crazy Cat Lady path.

Okay, we didn't actually worry about the crazy cat lady thing. Much.

But to know that you are pursuing a relationship with a person that we already love and know to be an amazing lady just makes us very proud and very happy.

And the tears are only for knowing this has cost you in ways it should not.

And I wondered if there have been points along the way when I could have made it easier and just didn't know how. You know that I believe Master Parenting is managing the environment your child lives in, versus managing your child.

And this time, I am powerless in the face of some of what I know will come your way. Just wish I could change the world. I wouldn't change a single thing about you.

Tell Erica cookies and cannons is December 17 and no fair coming up with excuses. I have already checked the LSJU calendar and you will be done with classes :-) This represents my overbearing parenting.... EVERYBODY MUST EMBRACE THE BAKE.

Love, love, love you.

Mommy

On Oct 24, 2011, at 9:21 PM, Annie Graham <aegraham> wrote:

1) Fortunately there's still hope for me to be a crazy cat lady, but honestly I'd prefer to be a crazy guinea pig lady....when being a kooky old person, I say go big or go home.

2) You and John are just the best. Thanks for being the best.

3) SO EXCITED FOR COOKIE BAKE. Though I'd love for one of us to defy gender norms and go cannon shooting, Erica and I have mostly bonded over a mutual affinity for food and all things that have to do with food—would the Women of the World condone a love for baking? The cookie bake also reminds me that time is flying by and I should go study school things.

Love you and hope your travels are going well,

Annie

I need to explain just a few points there...first of all, our family has held a cookie bake event for about 27 years, after Pat and I started it shortly after we met. And John fought back a few years ago by buying a cannon he could shoot with some of the guys instead of baking cookies. Each to his own...I do enforce happy attendance at one or the other.

Next, Annie's allusion to Women of the World (WOW, to those in the know) is an uncharitable reminder of the fact that when I was at Stanford in the late 1970s, I helped to start an organization to empower women in the workplace. It had the cringe-worthy name you see there, and having discovered this fact, my children find a way to work it into most conversations.

What touches me most about what Annie said to me is this "...every time someone reacts well, or says really nice things, especially a parent, people cling to that and feel like this is okay and this is a viable thing and *this can be good for the world, just like any good relationship can.*"

I have no earthly idea why any committed, supportive relationship is not a plus for our children and for the world. Intimate relationships provide strength for our work and for offering service to others. They matter enormously. All of them.

So if you are the parent of somebody who tells you that they are lesbian, gay, bi-sexual, or transgender, then with all my heart I congratulate you on raising a person who has determined to live an honest life. That is heroic. You will fear for their ability to confront a world where too many people will indulge their own ignorance by mistreating your child. I do understand. But if your child has been clear enough about themselves and their purpose to share who they are with you and with others, you can be proud of raising a courageous and honest person. Be very, very happy about that. People need to know and love themselves in order to take on the purpose they are meant for.

The fact is, children find lots of ways to surprise us.

If you are the parent of a child who tells you that despite your hopes for them to pursue the law, they wish to pursue their art, then congratulations. Or likewise, if you are an artist with a child who wants to pursue the law, or you are a Republican with a child who wants to become an activist for Democrats...hooray! Your life just got interesting!

The point is, being somebody's parent means you are a primary partner in helping that person be the absolute best of who they are. You get to model good behavior, choose great schools, help develop physical and social skills and encourage service to others. What you don't get is to determine specifically who they are or who they will become.

That was never yours to decide...it is yours to celebrate as it happens. And what an amazing gift that is.

Chapter Nine

Guidepost Three

―※―

I suppose it is possible that we are all just here through some exquisite series of spiritually random events. I do not disparage this view, even though it is not something I hold as true. But regardless of what any of us believe about why we are here, or what brought us here, each of us is operating on some overarching expectation about our purpose. And you must know that, know what that is for you, or you will have a very difficult time putting your child's life into context for them…or for you.

Guidepost #3: Children need to see their lives and their work in a sacred context. And so do you.

Putting a child's life into a broad, meaningful, purposeful context is one the most important things anyone who cares for that child can accomplish for them. I can't and won't suggest a worldview for anyone else; I think everyone already has their own. But I do know mine well, and I believe that we are here, each one of us, to add value to the world, in ways that only our particular gifts can manage. This is why I have an obsessive commitment to the rights of people to be free to exercise their own gifts, in their own way, according to their own beliefs. I am humbled by the fact that life situated me in a family, community and country where that is possible.

This worldview that you have affects you deeply, and will affect your child even more. I am convinced that children who are raised to believe in and love themselves, to see their responsibility to serve others, to improve the lives of those around them, to commit themselves to a purpose far greater than their selfish happiness...have a much better shot at becoming wonderful members of their shared communities. Consequently, they have a better shot at their own happiness this way. It is, in my grandfather Pop's vernacular, a really Big Thing to consistently remind your child that he or she came here with a sacred purpose, and that together you will work to develop everything needed to act on that purpose.

It may be that you connect this to your faith; we certainly did that and believe a child's purpose is divinely inspired. But the act of encouraging a child in this way is nonsectarian: the child in your care has an important purpose that will be theirs alone to recognize and act on. Tell this to the child. And let that child know that one of your own life's biggest purposes is to be a parent or role model and to get them ready for their life. Tell them you are so happy about that because you know he or she was sent to do amazing things that will help other people. Make sure that this child knows it is a solemn privilege that you take very seriously.

Purpose should not be something we merely reflect on occasionally...in Sunday church services or over a glass of whiskey in the evening. Although I am all for either. Where children are concerned, purpose can be the guiding principle for how adults interact with them. It is nearly always possible to help a child see that every day holds its own possibilities for them to develop or act on their sacred purpose. Every interaction, every time the child is faced with learning something new, or appreciating something never seen or done before, or meeting somebody new...all of that is part of a meaningful life as it happens.

So this begins to sound exhausting.

What I am not suggesting is that parents and caregivers assign to themselves and their children a sort of grim list of daily do-gooder duties. This is not about a to-do list, it's about a lens. We must give children a lens through which they interpret life events and their place in the world from very early on.

All children learn to interpret what happens to them through some prism of understanding, whether or not they've had the benefit of guidance. And while it may sound like hyperbole to suggest that every daily interaction is somehow sacred, I guarantee that every interaction shapes a child. It takes work, but pay attention and choose to comment on the significant interactions you witness with children. Provide them with context and use the opportunity to let the child gain a constructive view of their place, their role and participation in that particular "teachable moment."

The lens you choose to give a child will directly shape the way they see the world. It's a huge responsibility. And it can't be a sometimes thing. Think about the way your child sees you respond to the world. Every day, all the time, in the little as well as the Big Things. What would you learn if *you* were watching you?

Here is how the lens works. If you choose to rail at small daily events that come your way, and your child constantly hears you depict yourself as a victim of events, you have chosen a negative lens through which your child will learn to view the world. If you are addicted to complaining rather than putting life's events into a broadly optimistic and purposeful context, then you must expect that your child will see through this lens as well.

Make the choice to help the child see events as potentially positive, and to see himself as a critical piece of the world as it happens, capable of influencing it toward the positive. Focusing on the positive does not make you a Pollyanna, incapable of appreciating the difficulty that life can pose. But it brings you down on the side of optimism. I suggest that searching for what is good, seeking the best in situations and people, will create a better opportunity for the children you influence.

Providing a hopeful context for the children, and assuring them of their own ability to influence events trains children to avoid becoming targets or victims. As an adult outside the observation of children, a habit of indulging in self-pity and self-centered whining doesn't really hurt anybody; it's more likely to annoy people and make them unwilling to sit next to the whiner at dinner.

But as a parent or role model, this negativity is very serious. Children learn what to expect from the world by observing us. We play out the roles that we observe most often. We become the person we see in ourselves at a very, very young age.

It is through the words and actions of adults that children learn to believe that everything they do and experience can be part of making the world a better, happier, more peaceful place for everybody. When they believe that, they are important already. That is a really Big Thing.

And it isn't easy to do this, even in the best circumstances. If any of us truly knew what it would take to help a child develop into a good and positive person, fully capable and intent on making their meaningful contribution to the world, we might decline parenthood altogether. But it is a miracle of the human condition that hope springs eternal, and we are inexplicably driven to bring children into our lives and our families.

So...how to do this on a daily basis? Well, short of being tutored in this by Daphne, it's difficult to describe what a positive lens looks like because there are so many moments in every day. Most of all, model what you want to see. Everything you say and do is being taken very seriously by the child who observes you. They bank your words and actions like cold, hard cash. And as they become adults and go to spend those words and actions, you want to make sure that the vault they withdraw from is mostly full of words and actions you would like to see coming back to the world.

Let's take just a few examples:

From the books you read: You know reading to a child is essential. Just as important is helping that child see himself or herself in those stories. When you are reading aloud, talk about how the characters do things that affect other people, and compare that to something the child did recently. For example, " Remember how the little mouse set the lion free from his trap? That mouse was so little, but he did a really big and important thing. That reminds me of how you helped GrandMommy take all of the dishes from the table and get them washed. I like how you help people get big things done."

When times are tough: When things go badly, you can provide positive context. For example, when a child is treated poorly by another child, obviously we must determine what happened to ensure this was child play versus bullying. But don't immediately leap to the negative. Work to see most events as what they are: simply life, awaiting interpretation. Put unhappy stuff into a happier context: "I am so sorry that Jane hurt you. That doesn't seem like something she meant to do, but it was wrong. Sometimes even our best friends do mean things, just like all of us do mean things sometimes. If our friends do mean things all the time, then we can't have them for friends anymore and that would be sad. Real friends like us to be happy and do good things. Jane probably just had a crabby day. Give her one more chance. Nobody likes to feel crabby."

Please compare that example of how to respond to playground mishaps to the far too common practice of threatening to sue the preschool. Amazing to me is the number of folks whose greatest gift appears to be whittling innocuous events into razor sharp arrows. Here's an optional way to behave: Accept the fact that escalation starts and stops with you. If an event can be interpreted as neutral, then by all means interpret it that way. Or better yet, assert the positive for your child.

There will be plenty of times when genuinely bad things happen and the situation must be managed. But please, please, please…go easy on the dramatic negative interpretation. There are so many moments in life that are simply that: moments. They don't really have much meaning until they've been assigned one. It's really all about that lens again, and the reaction to events is within an adult's power to manage. Just remember that a child is watching.

When considering our own children's bad behavior: Remember my uncle Bobby's advice? It pertains to our children too. They are composed of 25 percent—well, for kids, let's call it nonsense—and from time to time, they act with 100 percent of that 25 percent. There will be weeks when that's all you see, and it is easy to forget that there is a 75 percent good kid in there somewhere. Think of these times as primo learning opportunities. Once a child can accept that they can do bad things and still be good people, they can accept that in others as well.

The danger is that children test the limits of an adult's ability to believe there is anybody with a higher calling in that obnoxious little body. Keep believing, because the danger is always that you will forget yourself in these really trying moments. You risk demeaning the child by equating who they are with their nonsense, as in: "You are a very bad girl."

Nope. She is a good girl doing bad things.

Or, another danger emerges when you allow yourself the indulgence of making these trying moments about you, as in saying to a misbehaving child, "You are making me very sad right now."

Nope. She's not making you sad—even if she is. You have to fake it to stay strong in your adult role; you need to model strength and not succumb to your own frustration in a moment like this. Cry and yell in the bathroom later, but hold it in a bit until the discipline has been accomplished. This is really important: Children cannot be allowed to dictate their parents' happiness. That's too much power.

There are two things a child must absolutely know in order to appreciate themselves and their obligations:

They do have vast, sacred, inherent *value*.

They do not have vast, sacred, inherent *power*.

Adults must consistently encourage children to be the best they can be, just like adults work to be. And while supporting a child's best behavior and putting it in context for them, adults must also set the example for what a good grown-up looks like. And part of being a good grown-up is that you don't look like a child, and you don't get unreasonably influenced by a child.

Guidepost Three

Instead, allow a child to gradually assert their influence in slowly expanding environments. It is much easier to control the environment that your child occupies than it is to constantly attempt to control your child. Think of this as gradually expanding the size of your child's crib.

Parents can be obsessive about the crib. They want it to be comfortable, pretty and possibly to compliment the beautiful wall trim with matching curtains, lamps, light switches and mobiles. Which folks will understand if they indulged all those accessory obsessions. I might have. But above all, parents want that crib to be safe. It's the one place where the baby will be fine—if not thrilled, necessarily—while parents go take care of other things, or when it is time for them to go to sleep or simply have some time alone.

A good parent has controlled that total crib environment. Rails and posts were measured to prevent a head being stuck; the mattress is placed at the correct height; fluffy comforters, pillows, toys and other things that might suffocate a baby are out. Now, the baby will be safe in the crib and at liberty in there to do as she pleases, because the environment has been properly controlled.

Gradually, parents expand the number of places a child can be free to operate without restriction…to a playpen, then a den configured with safety plugs on outlets, sofas and pillows arranged to create a friendly prison of sorts. And we do that so that the child is free to experiment in ever more complex environments, slowly conquering new obstacles, and gaining control over impulses so that eventually their ability to judge the safety of an environment and navigate it substitutes for the adult having to control it.

The goal is for a child to develop a kind of safe independence, to be free to navigate in environments that can't threaten any danger. Yet, the environment cannot be so sheltered that it creates boredom or lacks challenge. A child's environment should be revised often to introduce more novelty, more risk, something new to conquer. That is how children

Simple Choices

develop a sense of how to manage the world around them. And how they grow to believe that they can.

A big part of this is teaching the child how to control the impulse to do things that would put them in danger in a less restrictive, more threatening environment. But impulse control is both learned and a function of absolute brain capacity…children get that over time, and caregiving adults can see it develop. Keep the child in a controlled environment, consistent with the ability to control themself.

I get just a little crazed watching parents allow their children to operate in an environment that is too risky for their impulse control. For example, they allow a child to crawl around a room with a fire in the fireplace, glasses on low coffee tables and unprotected outlets everywhere. And instead of making the child safe by putting her in a playpen or arranging furniture to create a friendly prison, the parent runs around yelling "NO!" and slapping a tiny hand every time the child—predictably, inevitably—reaches for a glass, an outlet, or a burning log.

Children must be taught how to navigate the world after an adult has made the world safe for navigation. Introduce new challenges and risks as the child conquers others, always offering novel adventures consistent with the ability they've already demonstrated. Allowing children to navigate an environment beyond limits they can manage frustrates everybody.

It is pretty easy to do this when the babies are small and arranging furniture is the task at hand. Arranging the environment for a child gets more complicated as they get older and grow confident. But continually managing their environments is essential. As your child gets old enough to try and influence your parenting, it is tempting to allow them more liberty than they are ready to own.

This is tough stuff. But the reason not to allow a child to unreasonably influence you—the adult—is because it is just downright frightening for a child to have control over an adult. Allowing a child to have control over you can be as damaging as a jolt from an outlet. It just isn't safe, and you can't allow it.

Okay...brief sidebar. As I was writing these pieces of parent advice, a friend asked me what books I relied on when developing my personal rules. Which is an embarrassing question because I read enough to paralyze myself. So the answer is that I read nearly the entire section at the bookstore. My greatest influencer was not the words in those books, however, it was my mother, and I dearly wish I could bottle her methods. There are parenting experts—and then there are truly great parents. I am not a parenting expert, I am just passing on what I learned from one of the greats. Who I could never control, by the way, which brings us back to the subject at hand.

Children will act like they want control over you, because they want everything. If their tantrum can result in you changing your mind and giving in to a short term desire of theirs, what's not to love? For the moment.

But it cheats them of the security that boundaries provide, and they desperately need that. Children need the security of knowing they are supported and safe as they attempt ever more complex interactions, but they need to begin by applying their emerging abilities in very limited spheres of influence. You will sense their ability to handle more as time goes along. Having too much or too early control over things beyond their sphere is not healthy for them or for you. And it can be a serious emotional or intellectual inhibitor.

Instead of giving in to a child's demands, adults can introduce a larger environment for them to navigate by slowly allowing them more liberty in their choices. But be serious about this...*because choices really are very sacred things*. Getting to do what you want to do is a privilege; and a child's confidence in their choices should unfold and develop gradually and as they become capable.

So when you offer choices, mean it.

Simple Choices

Let me further explain. If you intend for your child to do something, if it is something that must get done, do *not* formulate this as a choice. Listening to parents present their children with choices that are not really choices frustrates me. Example: It is time to get in the car and go to school. And mom says, "Do you want to go to school now?"

Bad idea. Be declarative with your child when you don't intend to offer choices. "Time to go to school! Let's get in the car."

This starts very early with parents, and I am afraid it becomes habit. I suspect that parents feel they are being gentle by not forcing such situations on their children: "Do you want your bottle?" "Shall we put your shoes on?" "Do you want to go to bed now?"

Choices are magic things. They represent statements of who a person really is. Asserting a desire defines a person in the moment of choosing. Babies and children are not ready to decide what is right for themselves, so they cannot be allowed to make some choices they would like to make until they are capable, and more mature. Pretending to allow them that precious responsibility when you are not prepared to give it to them is both an emotional and developmental danger.

Questions have rules that even very small children understand. We get asked questions when somebody wants to know what we want, or what we think or feel, or what is on our mind…it puts the ball squarely in our court. Or it should. That is the purpose of a question. It's a tiny little contract between questioner and questionee. There are rules.

And so when you ask a child to do something that must be done, and the child says or indicates "No"…what's next?

Don't put the ball in the child's court if you intend to hop over the net and bat it back to yourself. It makes them resentful and then they lose trust in your intentions. Why did you even ask? They grasp this very, very early.

So instead of the outright, open-ended ask, do one of two things:

Guidepost Three

Be declarative, and simply state what is going to happen next. If the child doesn't want to do whatever is going to happen, feel free to offer your understanding. "I know, it's a bummer for you, but we are leaving now."

Offer a couple of choices if your child is old enough to choose. So maybe, "It's time to go to school, shall we put your shoes on right now, or when you get in the car?" The beauty of this limited choice is that it does allow your child to exercise some opinion, and to have gradually escalating control over situations. If you have time and energy to create these options, it's preferable. If not, just get on with the day!

The point is, be the decider when you need to be. And don't apologize for it.

The irony here is that children who exercise too much control over adults are not doing so out of an advanced maturity. Children who are allowed too much control will usually dictate terms to their parents in order to keep from experiencing the stress of novel situations. Nor will they develop the impulse control that is needed to balance what they want with the needs and demands of others. It takes a lot of energy for children to do either of those things. Don't underestimate how tough that is, instead, be proud as your child develops this essential control.

It's my experience that most people know children who control the adults in their lives. These kinds of children most often do not demonstrate much ease in novel situations. Like all of us, children find comfort in the familiar. If a child learns that hissy fits will manipulate his parents into providing everything he wants, why learn to risk new people and new environments?

Children need to be a bit uncomfortable and challenged in order to become independent, and confident of their ability to navigate. There's an adrenaline rush that comes with the novel experience, and children benefit from learning to manage that. They are especially driven to get this rush as they approach adolescence (it is a consequence of neural maturing) and you can create a very dangerous situation if you have not made a habit of allowing them to conquer novel situations. If kids are not engaged in tackling new experiences and getting the rush of satisfaction that provides, they will look for passive ways to gain that feeling. And as they get older, those passive ways too often involve drugs, alcohol or other maladaptive behaviors.

Be very deliberate about this if you are raising or influencing a child. Children need to get right up to the limits of what is safe or what is okay with their adult model and from time to time they need to cross over the limit, get the consequence and learn how that works. They fall off a chair, or they get disciplined, and they have to adapt. They learn.

Adults should be confident about defining but also revising a child's boundaries. Give them as much freedom as you can to safely experiment, but then be cheerful and clear about the discipline they earn for violating the rules. It's as essential as all of the praise that should be heaped on every child. I used to tell my kids that if they were going to ask to be disciplined, I would cooperate. They could count on me. And they could count on consequences.

I have very fond memories of sitting with my back against the door for what felt like hours in order to enforce a time-out for 3-year-old Annie after a serious infraction. If there had been such a thing as preschool boot-camp, I might have tried that with Annie. She had lots of opinions. Many of these hours were spent simultaneously on the phone with my mother, hoping for moral support as I was certain that my isolation techniques were going to subject me to home visits from local child welfare agents.

When Daphne answered my call she heard, "Oh good God, Mom. How did you do this? I feel like a child abuser, and if you could hear Annie screaming you would know what I mean."

"Honey, first of all, I *can* hear Annie screaming…will you please turn down the volume on your phone? And secondly, you forget I raised you. You turned out fine. Nobody likes a wimpy baby!"

My mother thinks a child's temper tantrums are a sign of mental health…within reason. She believes in an occasional exercising of the 25 percent. Plus, she tells me that I was so disenchanted with my inability to bend her to my will as a baby that I learned to hold my breath until I passed out. When she took me to the doctor, he indicated that she should walk out of the room when I did it, because once I passed out, I would start breathing again. So she did. Problem solved.

Our family tradition for children who are acting out is to isolate them, staying close enough to ensure their safety, but not close enough to allow them to affect us. The wilder they get, the calmer we are. My mother did believe in the business end of a wooden spoon when we were little, always administered lightly and dispassionately on the leg before the prison sentence. I learned to do the same thing…for serious infractions it was a lightly applied wooden spoon, followed by enforced isolation. All of this is a Daphne skill, honed to a fine art in my mother and I got pretty good at it over the years. I have to highly recommend some version of this kind of discipline. You may want to leave out the light wooden spoon option—I know folks have very strong feelings about these things and you have to do what you believe is best—but enforcing a time out enables you to enact a price for bad behavior while minimizing the chance of an escalating emotional engagement. In other words, no need to shout.

I get really sad when I watch parents in a shouting match with their small children. That is 100 percent a poor parenting decision. When a parent says "That's enough!" to a child, the parent needs to believe it and act on it. I suggest adopting a grim smiley face. Any child's attempt to invoke parental sadness and sympathy is lost with the appearance of the parental grim smiley face. You can almost hear the child's thinking: "How can you be happy when I am SO UNHAPPY???!!"

Having established an initial victory, it's time to move the child to a quiet room with a door on it. Then shut the door, with you on the other side of it. When out and about in public, a parent may need to get the child outside and make them sit, facing away from everyone or any distraction, for a short while. Long enough for the child—and the parent—to catch a breath and re-set the attitude.

During this time out, think pleasant thoughts. Think of your favorite comedy routines. Console yourself by knowing that you just created a favorite moment for the dozens of shoppers, church goers, and citizens who saw you haul a wailing and flailing toddler outside, all accomplished with a big grim smiley face. Hey, you'll be dinner conversation all over town! Most of all, remind yourself that this is how you shape good character and plan to treat yourself to a serious merit badge at the end of the day. I ate a lot of chocolate when my kids were little.

With my son Justin, we had to finesse the isolation-only time out technique a bit by taking toys away as punishment. Justin was a planner, and he learned to plant passive-aggressive bombs during his prison stays. He was always compliant when sent to his room as punishment, and in the days that followed I would discover little acts of toddler revolt such as torn pages in books or scribbling on the wall inside his closet.

Justin's all-time best was my discovery of an attack on the wall behind his bed which had apparently been going on for years. This Booger Offensive, launched during the times I believed he was quietly reflecting on his manifold sins, had been exercised with such artistry and precision that I needed a sander and professional painter to repair the wall when we moved. Justin was a patient baby with my father's sense of strategy: Don't get mad, get even.

So anyone's best-laid disciplinary programs have serious bugs. The point is to have them anyway.

Now, in real life there will be moments parents wish they could have back. As in a do-over. If you are experiencing this moment, you will not be the picture of calm; you will not be able to summon even a grim smiley face. You will find yourself literally screaming, chasing a very small person around a very large house. You will shout, you may cry, you will say things you desperately wish that you had not.

The best way through these moments is just to lean in to the truth of them. The truth is, you messed up. Adults and children should be able to learn from that as well. Just share the truth of the situation and your errors with the children. Remember, honest communication is always a great place to start. After the storm breaks and everyone has had some time to reflect, go to your child and explain that while what the child did was wrong, it was also wrong to have lost your temper. Do not lighten or remove punishment as a result (unless you got crazy about it) because that creates a situation where the child benefits from your bad behavior. That's wrong. A child's punishment relates to the child, not the adult. Let the child know that you believe it is your job to be their parent as happily as you can, and you are so sorry you failed at that in the given situation. Explain that sometimes you get angry and then act angry.

You should absolutely apologize, but for Heaven's sake don't look for children to offer you absolution or wait for their forgiveness. Adults apologize because that is the right thing to do when they behave badly. Seeking a child's absolution is another example of giving them too much power. Be gracious if it comes (do not ask for or expect it), but just make sure you are direct in the apology for your behavior, and then return the focus to them and the fact that you are glad to have the job of being their parent, even when it's a challenge for everybody!

Let me add a really important note here. If at any time you feel that you have the capacity to physically harm your child, or you possess an ability to say cruel and demeaning things, please know that is *never* right. It is way outside the boundaries of acceptable behavior, and an apology will not suffice. You need to seek help. There are many families where violence is a tragic tradition, and the only way to break that cycle is for an honest adult to go get help. You have to be that adult if this is your situation.

Another blessing in my life was growing up next door to my uncle, Dr. Kipp Charlton, who has been a leader in Maricopa County Hospital's pediatric care unit for nearly all of his adult life. And as part of that work, he enlisted the support of his wife, my aunt Susie, my mother and a number of their friends in creating the first Child Crisis Center for parents who either had harmed their children or felt that they might. It was both heartbreaking and hopeful to learn about these children and their families, and another early confirmation for me that one can always choose a better way. There are always people whose lives are dedicated to helping others make wise choices.

So if you need help, or if you know somebody who does, one phone call will put you in touch with a whole host of people who understand and want to work through any situation that presents danger.

There is a magic dance in the power struggle that is parent and child. Parents want to exercise enough control to prevent danger or to keep children from developing an overinflated sense of power, but they also want to allow children an emerging sense of their ability to impact the world. This can be done by consistently reminding them that all of their work and play is meant for the day they will be of great help to the world. And they can certainly appreciate that from very early on. They can know that is their job; they can know that is what the adults they love expect.

The point is to make sure that your child emerges from this early and very important period of their lives with confidence, respect and optimism about becoming everything they arrived in the world prepared to be.

Just being alive and part of any family or community is a really big, really important thing—and it is important children know this. Every child has enormous purpose. Helping children to see that and to understand how to be ready to participate…every day, in a myriad of tiny ways…is a parent's sacred mission.

Chapter Ten

Choosing the Future

I want to summarize my thoughts about guidelines for creating good environments for children by switching the conversation from character to intellect. I am one book away from talking to parents and guardians about choosing a great school for their child, and how to fight for the right to do so. But it is my fondest hope that parents will have excellent options in schooling available, and that those who are searching for a school will make it their business to go visit lots of schools, look online at the school scores and parent comments, (go to www.greatschools.net), and ask the school leadership why you should send your child to their school.

Anybody who thinks they deserve to have a child attend their school ought to be able to say why that is a good idea. In order to find a good fit, search the options…there are usually far more school choices than people know. And the pace at which new schools are coming on the market, both public and private, has never been faster. Keep yourself informed about this. Regardless of the school, I do want to make sure you can give your child the best possible start.

When it comes to education and the shaping of intellect, I am often surprised at how many parents feel as though there are just a few obvious basics that children need before school, and they will be good to go. All of us know that children need to understand how to approach books, be introduced to colors and shapes, and maybe start on learning the alphabet. But it is also critical that we see the intellect as something that can be shaped every day, exactly as behavior can be.

Simple Choices

It must be.

Shaping a child's intellect is similar to providing them with a lens or a perspective for how they understand their lives. But in the case of intellect, it is shaped first and foremost through language. Language gives children the structure by which they organize their thoughts—so that they can understand their lives, and the world around them. Language is not a single subject learned in school, and it isn't simply a baby's lovely first words.

Language is the meaning of life, translated. It is helpful to imagine language as translated thought, sitting in the brain in discreet little bricks of meaning, collecting neighbors, adding new words that will fit together and expand the road of intellect like pavers on a highway. And that is the best way to think of it: Language builds the road that ideas will one day travel down. It is everything to a child.

I am particularly obsessive about this because I was lucky enough to major in human language and language acquisition. This is what I understand and what I love, so there is my bias. But every parent should understand the compelling statistics about differences in future intellectual prowess based solely on the number of words preschoolers can use or understand when they enter school.

It is not true that children just show up with either good brains or bad brains, or that families with money automatically have kids who will be smarter than everybody else. I get so tired of having that discussion with people!

What is true, however, is that the very early development of the brain has a huge impact on its future usefulness. *And the things that build a brain are experiences translated into language.* Those of us who are enamored with linguistics as a pastime know there are about a gazillion hours' worth of reading on how this all comes about. It's fun—if you're a word and language geek. But for parents, they need only know that what a child sees or hears or experiences, explained by a loving adult, becomes meaningful via language. Language in all its glory...the words themselves, their multiple meanings, their use in and out of context, even the gestures and expressions that accompany verbal or signed words...all of that is what gives children the head start they need. Literally.

So here are some numbers to know:

By age three, your child should have a working vocabulary of about 1,000 words. Rest assured a vocabulary is not what a child *says*, it is what a child *knows*. So children will have much larger "receptive" language banks (what they understand) than they will "expressive" abilities (what they can say). Still, that's a lot of language. For those who are quick with math, that represents just under one word for every day a baby has been around.

In most cases, scientists start calculating language acquisition around age one, and anticipate that kids will pick up just under 2.5 words a day. Not literally—some days are more exciting than others. In houses where parents have professional degrees, kids are exposed to roughly 2,150 different words an hour when their parents are talking to other adults. When these same parents are talking directly to their babies, exposure drops to around 400 words an hour, and should. No infant can keep up with the pace of adult conversation, and we are all wired to slow it down and even change the tone of our voices when talking to babies and small children. It's universal, it's innate and it's necessary. Don't make fun of your friends' and partners' goofy baby voices...they are just going native. It works.

When children are first learning language, an adult can be of the most help by being a game show host to the game of life. I loved playing this role for my children. I got to be a constant commentator, pointing out what I saw for them, naming things as they appeared and then expanding on exciting or interesting aspects of what we were experiencing together. It was also fun to make up big crazy stories and encourage them to do the same. Children have such fertile imaginations; I was always amazed at how fluent and detailed their totally fabricated stories were. Children are just fabulous company no matter how old they get. I still play twenty questions with my adult children while bike riding or riding in a car. It's like working crossword puzzles…a good workout for everyone's grey matter.

Plus taking on this attitude of narrator for life reminds you that your child is always listening. Just because your child doesn't talk yet does not mean you shouldn't be "in conversation" anytime you are together. Introducing your child to the world, sharing your excitement about things that happen, uncovering small mysteries, discovering wonderful people…all of these things reflect an attitude on your part that tells your child you believe they are worth sharing these things with. I became very humbled by the fact that I was the person who was shaping how my children would view events, people, novelty. I could see that where I was nervous, they would be nervous, where I was happy and confident, they would be encouraged to be as well. Understanding the potential for every moment we were together to become a meaningful "paver" for my child kept me constantly engaged as a happy narrator.

Exposure to language play can be exhausting, but always a lot of fun, and it is without question the best possible way to develop your child's mind. Please do think of individual words as cobblestones or pavers that build roadways. Each word contributes further distance and gives a child more intellectual road to run on. Keep the image of a transportation grid in mind as you do this…it's helpful imagery as it truly reflects the kinds of connections that language creates in the brain.

As you name things for your child's benefit, expand their vocabularies by embellishing. It's one thing to say, "Oh, you have a ball." But you can amplify the power of those words by adding further context, as in: "Oh, you have a ball! That's a red ball. Shall we bounce the ball?" And silly always induces a better memory than straight-forward explanation. Putting the ball on your head is more memorable than simply describing it. By all means enjoy this process; it's more productive for everybody.

By playing with the word "ball" (Let's *bounce* the ball; Can I *bounce* it off your tummy? Will the ball *stay* on mommy's head or does it *roll off?*") the word becomes not just one paver, it attaches to other word-pavers. When you do this with common words, they will not only get used a lot, they will connect to lots of other words. So think of these as pavers with connecting joints. The more words a child collects that also serve as joints to other words, the better his intellectual road system is. Not only does it go far, but it goes in many different directions.

The same thing is true for a child's ability to collect words that are close in meaning but not exactly alike. In our family, these conversations were highlighted by the word "actually." If one of my kids said, "She looks happy," I would respond, "Yes, she looks happy, and *actually* I think she is even thrilled!" That kind of precision became a hallmark of my conversations with Annie and Justin to the point that "Actually, Mommy..." is what I remember most about talking with them at an early age. While I admire their conversational skills as adults, I have been hoisted on this linguistic petard of mine more than once. They are precise.

But it's worth it. Encourage children to understand that even small differences create powerful changes in meaning. Nuanced conversation is a highly sophisticated ability, and a wonderful thing to teach your child. Think of nuanced words as the beautiful little lanes that travel off of the main road. You don't have to take them, but life is a lot more creative and meaningful out there.

Gaining words at a strong pace allows a child's brain to lay down the communication roadway they will use all of their lives. The rapid period of language acquisition from birth to 7 years is phenomenal, and cannot be compensated for if we miss the opportunity. As kids grow older, they focus on connections between the ideas that they already know, becoming ever more sophisticated and adding depth and complexity to their foundations. But if they did not develop strong foundations, they lack a strong ability to connect. New ideas just can't find a ready home. It is very, very difficult for a child without sufficient language foundation to learn what he needs to know.

Which is why the following numbers should both shock and inspire you:

In homes where parents have college degrees, three-year olds know about 1,000 words. The differences between degree-earning parents and parents who have not been able to attain a college degree are stark. That figure for three-year old kids drops from 1,000 words down to about 750. And in homes where a family's income qualifies them for welfare assistance, that number is 500 words or less at three-years old.

Knowing this should serve only as motivation to fix it. Nothing that we know about language acquisition says that any normally developing child could not develop strong language foundation if exposed to enough of it. Learning all that is possible happens when children learn well from day one. And all adults with children in their care can be a part of making sure that happens.

By all means, be a word fanatic when you are interacting with any child. It's difficult to talk your way through a grocery store, a car ride home, a tour around the yard, and while making dinner. But the only way for children to build pathways of words, and meaning and intellect…is to listen to the speech of someone who loves them. Make sure you offer miles and miles of paving.

So while I don't want to get too far down this path, I could not end this story without paying homage to words and language, which I believe are keys to expressing the spirit. Who each of us "is" depends on a mysterious combination of biology, experience, spirituality, environment, and much else we can't know. What I obsess on, however, is providing our children with *what we do know* will help them step fully and confidently into who they were created to be. There is nothing simple about this, of course, but there is also nothing overly complex. We have to *see* the potential in children, *believe* in it, and *dedicate ourselves* to unleashing that magical person they were sent to be.

I am in love with a poem by Shel Silverstein that Pat used to have hanging in her office when we worked together at the VA Medical Center:

A Light In the Attic
There's a light on in the attic.
Though the house is dark and shuttered,
I can see a flickerin' flutter,
And I know what it's about.
There's a light on in the attic.
I can see it from the outside,
And I know you're on the inside... lookin' out.

My commitment to adults owing children their best effort reflects an intense belief on my part that each of us is created to be exceptional. We are meant to be. And we should make sure that we develop a child's ability to become this exceptional person, which sometimes means we have to trust Sol Silverstein's "flickerin' flutter" and to encourage others to do the same.

Look for a child to be fascinating, intelligent, original, a positive force for good. Be bold enough to see yourself in the same way, and seek to see or help develop that in others.

Children grow up fast. And as they reach school age their parents and guardians face critically important decisions about who gets to partner with them on raising and teaching their child. That is killer tough stuff, and it requires an ongoing focus on first principles: Choose a school where the child will be loved, respected and pushed to become fascinating, intelligent, original, and their best selves. Don't settle for good enough, don't assume exceptional isn't possible.

This is a serious challenge in our beautiful country, and very few of us can assume the local school will be a great fit. I hope you know that most American schools do not offer an internationally competitive level of academic challenge. Let me be very specific as this is difficult and merits an exact citation: The Organisation for Economic Co-operation and Development sponsors a regular international examination of 15 year old students in 70 different countries, known as the PISA, or the Programme for International Student Assessment. As of this year, the

United States ranks 14 of 34 OECD countries tested in reading, 17th in science, and a very disappointing 25th in math. That lack of achievement is the reason for the urgent push for school reform, and for the national discussion about a "Common Core" of academic standards that all states would voluntarily agree to adopt. There are many answers available, but none so compelling to me as to look to excellent teachers for solutions.

And I believe in that solution because I see visionary teachers transform lives. Over and over again.

The great privilege of my work is that it allows me to spend the majority of my time connecting with many of the stellar teachers and policy makers who believe that excellence in education is always possible…everywhere, for every child, regardless of wealth, social status, ethnicity, or family history. They spend every single day guiding young people into being everything they were meant to be. These innovative education leaders have created some of the most amazing, novel and successful school environments the country has ever seen.

Some of these educators have built schools or networks of schools that recruit children from very low-income neighborhoods where the education tradition for the past 50 years has been failure. But they orient themselves around what they believe is possible. And what they believe is possible transforms the lives of the young people in their schools. They do this via very hard work, lots of time, and lots of talent…but that is the 'how.'

The 'why' is because they see the children's potential. They see children honestly; they assume nothing but the good. They see fascinating, intelligent, original, the best each child has to offer. And they figure out how to help these children see that in themselves—or maybe more precisely to see that *as* themselves. Consequently, these children proceed to graduate high school, then attend and graduate from college. In recent years, I have watched as some of the students from these early public charter school networks have not only been the first in their family to graduate from college, but have become teachers and started teaching at the schools that inspired them.

These schools that transform children, families, and the communities they belong to are my greatest source of inspiration.

There are an incredible number of exceptional schools in our country, and they have the common features of being inspired by a compelling vision, and making sure that vision is translated into measurable goals that are measured and met. None of us as parents have the security of knowing that our children will attend one of these exceptional schools, we must choose carefully. Excellence abides in all types of schools…in the public district schools most of us attended, in public magnet schools, public charter schools, private schools, religious schools, home schools and online schools. I always tell parents enrolling their children in school for the first time or in a new community that if they can, they should visit at least 3-5 schools, making sure to visit at least two schools rated an "A" by the state or given a stellar rating by an organization like GreatSchools (greatschools.org). It is also instructive to visit a school or two that have a horrible rating, because understanding the difference in "feel" of those schools is important.

Schools are communities of people, and they reflect what the people in that community believe. Work to understand how a school sees your child, what they hope to accomplish for your child and with you. Choose a school that promises to challenge your child and you to push for excellence in academics, arts and sports, and in character.

It is no mystery to me why I want our absolutely brilliant teachers to have far more legal authority and freedom to create and manage schools. I believe trusting them to lead a positive revolution is working in several communities across the country, and I think these exceptional schools recover the potential of children to flourish. Belief in the miraculous capacity of our children drives fabulous educators to take over or to create schools worthy of a child's potential. Understanding what these leaders are capable of creating is essential for the next wave of public policies that can support them.

Which is an essential piece of what I do. My work to develop excellent school choices is just an obvious extension of my belief that every child in the world brings unique and inestimable value to the world. I will do everything in my power not to throw that potential away.

In the near future I will finish writing my book about all things school choice—most importantly about the people who provide it and how we find them for our children. It has been a difficult book for me to write, because the weight of it burdens me, and I know how distorted the national conversation about school choices can be.

The most honest national conversation we have about school choice takes place every January when millions of folks around the country celebrate National School Choice Week. And it is honest because the celebration is not about a particular tactic or brand or type of school. It is much bigger than that. It is a week-long party that shines a spotlight on the teachers who create excellent schools, the advocates who work for parent empowerment, and the parents who seek to choose the right schools for their children.

First of all, I love it because it's an all-inclusive party that includes all types of public and private schools, all political parties, and people who may only share this one belief in the power of excellent choices in schooling. National School Choice Week means everybody working together on a massive national party and I *love* when everybody gets along. But in the midst of the party, a beautiful story emerges of people struggling to do the right thing on behalf of children. I pray I will be able to tell their stories as well as my own.

I wanted to tell my story first because I believe it is right to know the heart and the intention of the guy or gal standing next to you in the battle, and I am hoping we are fighting together. It matters enormously who we are and what we hope for, and my life is massively blessed by the colleagues I work to support. Often I do not share their political views, often our personal histories are wildly different. But I know without a doubt that we share common ground in the hope for our children, and for the children all around us. Writing about my own experience with children, and about the family and friends who walk through life with me has been a joy, and I am deeply grateful to all of them for allowing me to tell a bit about their story as part of my own.

This book has a hole in it, however.

I described for you several times my gift of friendship with Pat—my children's aunt Pat. Well, actually she was everybody's aunt Pat. Over the years, most of what I wrote was edited or commented on by Pat. She was editing this book for me as well.

One of the reasons Pat could edit for me is because as any best friend will…she always told me the truth. But she also did more than edit. Pat could project for me what my writing would say to those who read it. She was good at understanding what others would hear that I did not think I was saying. As you know, she was a world class communicator …who did what it took to get a message across.

In the middle of summer in 2012, I took a call from Pat's husband Bernd on my birthday. And he was burdened with the horrible responsibility of telling me that Pat was going to die. The headaches that had plagued her in the spring turned out to be lung cancer which had travelled to her brain and elsewhere—something we did not discover until she was visiting her sister in July in Oregon. When they finally diagnosed the cancer, she was literally two weeks away from leaving us.

That simply was not supposed to happen. I don't collect best friends and Pat was as close to me as any person I have ever known, save my husband. I was lost. I have not navigated my life without Pat since I was 22 years old; it never occurred to me that I would have to. But I should have known, really. Pat was 18 years older than I am and we were both critically aware that we were not going to live forever. When we worked at the VA medical center, we used to joke that we wanted tattoos on our chests that read : "Do not resuscitate. And don't dress me up."

The dressing up thing was because we both abhorred the practice of putting Halloween costume bunny ears or devil horns on the men and women who had led our nation's military. Disrespectful doesn't quite capture it.

And having worked with so many people at the end of their lives, Pat and I learned to value the amazing beauty of life as we are free to live it while healthy. We saw a lot of pain in attempts to extend life beyond what seemed to be a compassionate end, and we didn't want that. Plus we were success junkies. Our shared obsession was being seen as competent, and that extended to our views on death. We had long ago decided that a great final line on a *lengthy* tombstone tribute for us would be: "She died really well."

But that was all in the abstract. Even though she got all of her departing wishes, the reality of life without Pat is starkly concrete. So I miss her and her honesty desperately and I feel the pain of this loss for my children. She was every bit another mother to all of them.

Yet I am also grateful for the call I didn't want, because Annie and I were able to fly to her right away, and to be there when her doctors shared this unwelcome news with her. She was present, and at peace, and just absolutely amazing. Pat had been working on a Tibetan singing bowl course all year, because she wanted more ability to let go of old issues. The singing bowl practice encourages people to use these beautiful melodic tones as a way to allow life's truths to simply be. It occurred to me that she aced the course.

I feel as though I should apologize to you that Pat left early. You may be reading things in the book that I am actually not trying to say, as she is not here to filter for me. But I think I was getting it right in her eyes—and ears. The last thing she emailed to me about the book was so typically Pat and something only she could say to me. Nobody else would dare: "Keep writing. I admire that you can put it in your words—not the way you might want the world to see you!"

You hear that too, right? Basically, she thinks I am a risk taker to let people see who I really am. She would know.

It took me a few months to get back on track and finish this without her. I apologize for what may be lacking here, but I also trust the wisdom in the world that brought her into my life in the first place, and taught me what I needed to know. She would never leave before we had shared all we were supposed to; so this book is as it was meant to be. Nobody would understand that better than Pat.

Thank you so much for giving the time you took to read through this. I honor that, and I hope you discovered something in my words—and her edits—that will be of lasting value for you.

I wish you and the children in your world an abundance of lovely, simple choices, and all of the magic that life has to offer.

About the Author

Lisa Graham Keegan has a passion for family - her family and the families of those who strive for a better future for their children. Her refreshing approach to the issues of the modern family is rooted in her belief that we have the family we are given and the family we build, and that all families exist to support the unique gifts and purposes of each member.

Lisa grew up in Arizona, riding horses and learning about life in a family steeped in commitment to service. Lisa's family has been involved in political and community leadership locally and nationally for generations. She was educated at Stanford University and Arizona State University, worked as a speech pathologist specializing in brain injury at the VA hospital, then ran for and was elected to the Arizona legislature and subsequently as Arizona Superintendent of Public Instruction. Lisa became a nationally recognized authority on what is right and what is wrong with education in America, and has advised policy leaders at all levels, from school boards to the White House.

In the course of her work, Lisa worked on both of John McCain's presidential campaigns, leading his education policy team. She also worked on the George W. Bush transition team in 2000, and was interviewed by President-elect Bush to be his Secretary of Education before the president chose Roderick Paige to take the job – a choice Lisa heartily approved of.

She shares ownership in the Keegan Company with her husband John, a former military officer, civil engineer, legislator, mayor and judge. Lisa's work includes analyzing education policy, giving advice, writing and speaking; and her favorite work obsession is National School Choice Week. She serves on numerous boards, including The Century Council which fights drunk driving and underage drinking, the Arizona Charter School Association, the National Alliance of Charter School Authorizers, and Teach for America in Phoenix. Lisa and John are also grateful members of the Episcopal diocese in Phoenix.

Her family life has been blessed with a close knit clan of children, stepchildren, children-in-law, grandchildren, former spouses, cousins, aunts, uncles and dear friends who come together to support each other as a family.

Lisa and John Keegan feel strongly about service to the community, believing that we are meant to improve the world through a disciplined focus on giving our best. The Keegans have five beautiful children, two children-in-law, two grandsons so far…and they are deeply proud of the contributions all of their children make to their own communities.